The Bernard Shaw Library

THE SHEWING-UP OF BLANCO POSNET

and

FANNY'S FIRST PLAY

Bernard Shaw was born in Dublin in 1856. Essentially shy, he created the persona of G.B.S., the showman, satirist, controversialist, critic, pundit, wit, intellectual buffoon and dramatist. Commentators brought a new adjective into English: Shavian, a term used to embody all his brilliant qualities.

After his arrival in London in 1876 he became an active Socialist and a brilliant platform speaker. He wrote on many social aspects of the day: on *Commonsense about the War* (1914), *How to Settle the Irish Question* (1917) and *The Intelligent Woman's Guide to Socialism and Capitalism* (1928). He undertook his own education at the British Museum and consequently became keenly interested in cultural subjects. Thus his prolific output included music, art and theatre reviews, which were collected into several volumes, such as *Music in London 1890–1894* (3 vols., 1931); *Pen Portraits and Reviews* (1931); and *Our Theatres in the Nineties* (3 vols., 1931). He also wrote five novels.

He conducted a strong attack on the London theatre and was closely associated with the intellectual revival of British theatre. His many plays fall into several categories: 'Plays Pleasant'; 'Plays Unpleasant'; his comedies; chronicle-plays; 'metabiological Pentateuch' (*Back to Methuselah*, a series of plays) and 'political extravaganzas'. G.B.S. died in 1950.

BERNARD SHAW

THE SHEWING-UP OF BLANCO POSNET

and

FANNY'S FIRST PLAY

DEFINITIVE TEXT
under the editorial supervision of
Dan H. Laurence

Penguin Books

Penguin Books Ltd, Harmondsworth, Middlesex, England
Viking Penguin Inc., 40 West 23rd Street, New York, New York 10010, USA
Penguin Books Australia Ltd, Ringwood, Victoria, Australia
Penguin Books Canada Ltd, 2801 John Street, Markham, Ontario, Canada L3R 1B4
Penguin Books (NZ) Ltd, 182–190 Wairau Road, Auckland 10, New Zealand

The Shewing-up of Blanco Posnet privately printed in 1909;
first published in English in 1911
First published in Penguin Books, in *Selected One Act Plays*, 1965

Fanny's First Play first published in English in 1914
First published in Penguin Books 1987

Published in one volume in Penguin Books 1987

Filmset in Baskerville, Linotron 202 by
Rowland Phototypesetting Ltd
Bury St Edmunds, Suffolk
Made and printed in Great Britain by
Cox & Wyman Ltd, Reading

Contents

THE SHEWING-UP OF BLANCO POSNET: A SERMON IN CRUDE MELODRAMA

WITH

Preface

Composition begun 16 February 1909; completed 8 March 1909. Privately printed for copyright in London and New York, 1909. First published in German translation, as *Blanco Posnets Erweckung*, in *Der Merker*, 25 October–25 November 1909. First published in English in *The Doctor's Dilemma, Getting Married, & The Shewing-up of Blanco Posnet*, 1911. Revised text in Collected Edition, 1930. First presented at the Abbey Theatre, Dublin, on 25 August 1909.

Babsy *Eileen O'Doherty*
Lottie *Cathleen Mullamphy*
Hannah *Sheila O'Sullivan*
Jessie *Mary Nairn*
Emma *Annie O'Hynes*
Elder Daniels *Arthur Sinclair*
Blanco Posnet *Fred O'Donovan*
Strapper Kemp *J. M. Kerrigan*
Feemy Evans *Sara Allgood*
Sheriff Kemp *Sydney J. Morgan*
Foreman of Jury *J. A. O'Rourke*
Nestor, a Juryman *A. J. Goulden*
The Woman *Maire O'Neill*
Waggoner Jo *Eric Gorman*

Period – 19th century

Scene – *A Town Hall in a Territory of the United States of America*

Preface

Contents

THE CENSORSHIP

This little play is really a religious tract in dramatic form. If our silly censorship would permit its performance, it might possibly help to set right-side-up the perverted conscience and re-invigorate the starved self-respect of our considerable class of loose-lived playgoers whose point of honor is to deride all official and conventional sermons. As it is, it only gives me an opportunity of telling the story of the Select Committee of both Houses of Parliament which sat last year to inquire into the working of the censorship, against which it was alleged by myself and others that as its imbecility and mischievousness could not be fully illustrated within the limits of decorum imposed on the press, it could only be dealt with by a parliamentary body subject to no such limits.

A READABLE BLUEBOOK

Few books of the year 1909 can have been cheaper and more entertaining than the report of this Committee. Its full title is REPORT FROM THE JOINT SELECT COMMITTEE OF THE HOUSE OF LORDS AND THE HOUSE OF COMMONS ON THE STAGE PLAYS (CENSORSHIP) TOGETHER WITH THE PROCEEDINGS OF THE COMMITTEE, MINUTES OF EVIDENCE, AND APPENDICES. What the phrase 'the Stage Plays' means in this title I do not know; nor does anyone else. The number of the Bluebook is 214. How interesting it is may be judged from the fact that it contains verbatim reports of long and animated interviews between the Committee and such witnesses as Mr William Archer, Mr Granville Barker, Mr J. M. Barrie, Mr Forbes Robertson, Mr Cecil Raleigh, Mr John Galsworthy, Mr Laurence Housman, Sir Herbert Beerbohm Tree, Mr W. L. Courtney, Sir William Gilbert, Mr A. B. Walkley, Miss Lena Ashwell, Professor Gilbert Murray, Mr George Alexander, Mr George Edwardes, Mr Comyns Carr, the Speaker of the House of Commons, the Bishop of Southwark, Mr Hall Caine, Mr Israel Zangwill, Sir Squire Bancroft, Sir Arthur Pinero, and Mr Gilbert Chesterton, not to mention myself and a number of gentlemen less well known to the general public, but important in the world of the theatre. The publication of a book by so many famous contributors would be beyond the means of any commercial publishing firm. His Majesty's Stationery Office sells it to all comers by weight at the very reasonable price of three-and-threepence a copy.

HOW NOT TO DO IT

It was pointed out by Charles Dickens in Little Dorrit, which remains the most accurate and penetrating study of the genteel littleness of our class governments in the English language, that whenever an abuse becomes oppressive enough to persuade our party parliamentarians that something must be done, they immediately set to work to face the situation and discover How Not To Do It. Since Dickens's day the exposures effected by the Socialists have so shattered the self-satisfaction of modern commercial civilization that it is no longer difficult to convince our governments that something must be done, even to the extent of attempts at a reconstruction of civilization on a thoroughly uncommercial basis. Consequently, the first part of the process described by Dickens: that in which the reformers were snubbed by front bench demonstrations that the administrative departments were consuming miles of red tape in the correctest forms of activity, and that everything was for the best in the best of all possible worlds, is out of fashion; and we are in that other phase, familiarized by the history of the French Revolution, in which the primary assumption is that the country is in danger, and that the first duty of all parties, politicians, and governments is to save it. But as the effect of this is to give governments a great many more things to do, it also gives a powerful stimulus to the art of How Not To Do Them: that is to say, the art of contriving methods of reform which will leave matters exactly as they are.

The report of the Joint Select Committee is a capital illustration of this tendency. The case against the censorship was overwhelming; and the defence was more damaging to it than no defence at all could have been. Even had this not been so, the mere caprice of opinion had turned against the institution; and a reform was expected, evidence or no evidence. Therefore the Committee was unanimous as to the necessity of reforming the censorship; only, unfortunately, the majority attached to this unanimity the usual condition that nothing should be done to disturb the existing state of things. How this was effected may be gathered from the recommendations finally agreed on, which are as follows.

1. The drama is to be set entirely free by the abolition of the existing obligation to procure a licence from the Censor before performing a play; but every theatre lease is in future to be construed as if it contained a clause giving the landlord power to break it and evict the lessee if he produces a play without first obtaining the usual licence from the Lord Chamberlain.

2. Some of the plays licensed by the Lord Chamberlain are so vicious that their present practical immunity from prosecution must be put an end to; but no manager who procures the Lord Chamberlain's licence for a play can be punished in any way for producing it, though a special tribunal may order him to discontinue the performance; and even this order must not be recorded to his disadvantage on the licence of his theatre, nor may it be given as a judicial reason for cancelling that licence.

3. Authors and managers producing plays without first obtaining the usual licence from the Lord Chamberlain shall be perfectly free to do so, and shall be at no disadvantage compared to those who follow the existing practice, except that they may be punished, have the licences of their theatres endorsed and cancelled, and have the performance stopped pending the proceedings without compensation in the event of the proceedings ending in their acquittal.

4. Authors are to be rescued from their present subjection to an irresponsible secret tribunal which can condemn their plays without giving reasons, by the substitution for that tribunal of a Committee of the Privy Council, which is to be the final authority on the fitness of a play for representation; and this Committee is to sit *in camera* if and when it pleases.

5. The power to impose a veto on the production of plays is to be abolished because it may hinder the growth of a great national drama; but the Office of Examiner of Plays shall be continued; and the Lord Chamberlain shall retain his present powers to license

plays, but shall be made responsible to Parliament to the extent of making it possible to ask questions there concerning his proceedings, especially now that members have discovered a method of doing this indirectly.

And so on, and so forth. The thing is to be done; and it is not to be done. Everything is to be changed and nothing is to be changed. The problem is to be faced and the solution to be shirked. And the word of Dickens is to be justified.

THE STORY OF THE JOINT SELECT COMMITTEE

Let me now tell the story of the Committee in greater detail, partly as a contribution to history; partly because, like most true stories, it is more amusing than the official story.

All commissions of public enquiry are more or less intimidated both by the interests on which they have to sit in judgment and, when their members are party politicians, by the votes at the back of those interests; but this unfortunate Committee sat under a quite exceptional cross fire. First, there was the king. The Censor is a member of his household retinue; and as a king's retinue has to be jealously guarded to avoid curtailment of the royal state no matter what may be the function of the particular retainer threatened, nothing but an express royal intimation to the contrary, which is a constitutional impossibility, could have relieved the Committee from the fear of displeasing the king by any proposal to abolish the censorship of the Lord Chamberlain. Now all the lords on the Committee and some of the commoners could have been wiped out of society (in their sense of the word) by the slightest intimation that the king would prefer not to meet them; and this was a heavy risk to run on the chance of 'a great and serious national drama' ensuing on the removal of the Lord Chamberlain's veto on Mrs Warren's Profession. Second, there was the Nonconformist conscience, holding the Liberal Government responsible for the Committee it had appointed, and holding also, to the extent of votes enough to turn the scale in some constituencies, that the theatre is the gate of hell, to be tolerated, as vice is tolerated, only because the power to suppress it could not be given to any public body without too serious an interference with certain Liberal traditions of liberty which are still useful to Nonconformists in other directions. Third, there was the commercial interest of the theatrical managers and their syndicates of backers in the City, to whom, as I shall shew later on, the censorship affords a cheap insurance of enormous value. Fourth, there was the powerful interest of the trade in intoxicating liquors, fiercely determined to resist any extension of the authority of teetotaller-led local governing bodies over theatres. Fifth, there were the playwrights, without political power, but with a very close natural monopoly of a talent not only for play-writing but for satirical polemics. And since every interest has its opposition, all these influences had created hostile bodies by the operation of the mere impulse to contradict them, always strong in English human nature.

WHY THE MANAGERS LOVE THE CENSORSHIP

The only one of these influences which seems to be generally misunderstood is that of the managers. It has been assumed repeatedly that managers and authors are affected in the same way by the censorship. When a prominent author protests against the censorship, his opinion is supposed to be balanced by that of some prominent manager who declares that the censorship is the mainstay of the theatre, and his relations with the Lord Chamberlain and the Examiner of Plays a cherished privilege and an inexhaustible joy. The error was not removed by the evidence given before the Joint Select Committee. The managers did not make their case clear there, partly because they did not understand it, and partly because their most eminent witnesses were not personally affected by it, and would not condescend to plead it, feeling themselves, on the contrary, compelled by their self-respect to admit and even emphasize the fact that the Lord Chamberlain in the exercise of his duties as licenser had done those things which he ought not to have done, and left undone those things which he ought to have done. Mr Forbes Robertson and Sir Herbert Tree, for instance, had never felt the real disadvantage of which managers have to complain. This disadvantage was not put directly to the Committee;

and though the managers are against me on the question of the censorship, I will now put their case for them as they should have put it themselves, and as it can be read between the lines of their evidence when once the reader has the clue.

The manager of a theatre is a man of business. He is not an expert in politics, religion, art, literature, philosophy, or law. He calls in a playwright just as he calls in a doctor, or consults a lawyer, or engages an architect, depending on the playwright's reputation and past achievements for a satisfactory result. A play by an unknown man may attract him sufficiently to induce him to give that unknown man a trial; but this does not occur often enough to be taken into account: his normal course is to resort to a well-known author and take (mostly with misgiving) what he gets from him. Now this does not cause any anxiety to Mr Forbes Robertson and Sir Herbert Tree, because they are only incidentally managers and men of business: primarily they are highly cultivated artists, quite capable of judging for themselves anything that the most abstruse playwright is likely to put before them. But the plain-sailing tradesman who must be taken as the typical manager (for the west end of London is not the whole theatrical world) is by no means equally qualified to judge whether a play is safe from prosecution or not. He may not understand it, may not like it, may not know what the author is driving at, may have no knowledge of the ethical, political, and sectarian controversies which may form the intellectual fabric of the play, and may honestly see nothing but an ordinary 'character part' in a stage figure which may be a libellous and unmistakable caricature of some eminent living person of whom he has never heard. Yet if he produces the play he is legally responsible just as if he had written it himself. Without protection he may find himself in the dock answering a charge of blasphemous libel, seditious libel, obscene libel, or all three together, not to mention the possibility of a private action for defamatory libel. His sole refuge is the opinion of the Examiner of Plays, his sole protection the licence of the Lord Chamberlain. A refusal to license does not hurt him, because he can produce another play: it is the author who suffers. The granting of the licence practically places him above the law; for though it may be legally possible to prosecute a licensed play, nobody ever dreams of doing it. The really responsible person, the Lord Chamberlain, could not be put into the dock; and the manager could not decently be convicted when he could produce in his defence a certificate from the chief officer of the King's Household that the play was a proper one.

A TWO GUINEA INSURANCE POLICY

The censorship, then, provides the manager, at the negligible premium of two guineas per play, with an effective insurance against the author getting him into trouble, and a complete relief from all conscientious responsibility for the character of the entertainment at his theatre. Under such circumstances, managers would be more than human if they did not regard the censorship as their most valuable privilege. This is the simple explanation of the rally of the managers and their Associations to the defence of the censorship, of their reiterated resolutions of confidence in the Lord Chamberlain, of their presentations of plate, and, generally, of their enthusiastic contentment with the present system, all in such startling contrast to the denunciations of the censorship by the authors. It also explains why the managerial witnesses who had least to fear from the Censor were the most reluctant in his defence, whilst those whose practice it is to strain his indulgence to the utmost were almost rapturous in his praise. There would be absolute unanimity among the managers in favor of the censorship if they were all simply tradesmen. Even those actor-managers who made no secret before the Committee of their contempt for the present operation of the censorship, and their indignation at being handed over to a domestic official as casual servants of a specially disorderly kind, demanded, not the abolition of the institution, but such a reform as might make it consistent with their dignity and unobstructive to their higher artistic aims. Feeling no personal need for protection against the author, they perhaps forgot the plight of many a manager to whom the modern advanced drama is so much Greek; but they did feel very strongly the need of being protected against Vigilance Societies and Municipalities and common informers in a country where a large section of the community still believes that art of all kinds is inherently sinful.

WHY THE GOVERNMENT INTERFERED

It may now be asked how a Liberal government had been persuaded to meddle at all with a question in which so many conflicting interests were involved, and which had probably no electoral value whatever. Many simple souls believed that it was because certain severely virtuous plays by Ibsen, by M. Brieux, by Mr Granville Barker, and by me, were suppressed by the censorship, whilst plays of a scandalous character were licensed without demur. No doubt this influenced public opinion; but those who imagine that it could influence British governments little know how remote from public opinion and how full of their own little family and party affairs British governments, both Liberal and Unionist, still are. The censorship scandal had existed for years without any parliamentary action being taken in the matter, and might have existed for as many more had it not happened in 1906 that Mr Robert Vernon Harcourt entered parliament as a member of the Liberal Party, of which his father had been one of the leaders during the Gladstone era. Mr Harcourt was thus a young man marked out for office both by his parentage and his unquestionable social position as one of the governing class. Also, and this was much less usual, he was brilliantly clever, and was the author of a couple of plays of remarkable promise. Mr Harcourt informed his leaders that he was going to take up the subject of the censorship. The leaders, recognizing his hereditary right to a parliamentary canter of some sort as a prelude to his public career, and finding that all the clever people seemed to be agreed that the censorship was an anti-Liberal institution and an abominable nuisance to boot, indulged him by appointing a Select Committee of both Houses to investigate the subject. The then Chancellor of the Duchy of Lancaster, Mr Herbert Samuel (now Postmaster-General), who had made his way into the Cabinet twenty years ahead of the usual age, was made Chairman. Mr Robert Harcourt himself was of course a member. With him, representing the

Commons, were Mr Alfred Mason, a man of letters who had won a seat in parliament as offhandedly as he has since discarded it, or as he once appeared on the stage to help me out of a difficulty in casting Arms and the Man when that piece was the newest thing in the advanced drama. There was Mr Hugh Law, an Irish member, son of an Irish Chancellor, presenting a keen and joyous front to English intellectual sloth. Above all, there was Colonel Lockwood to represent at one stroke the Opposition and the average popular man. This he did by standing up gallantly for the Censor, to whose support the Opposition was in no way committed, and by visibly defying the most cherished conventions of the average man with a bunch of carnations in his buttonhole as large as a dinner-plate, which would have made a Bunthorne blench, and which very nearly did make Mr Granville Barker (who has an antipathy to the scent of carnations) faint.

THE PEERS ON THE JOINT SELECT COMMITTEE

The House of Lords then proceeded to its selection. As fashionable drama in Paris and London concerns itself almost exclusively with adultery, the first choice fell on Lord Gorell, who had for many years presided over the Divorce Court. Lord Plymouth, who had been Chairman to the Shakespear Memorial project (now merged in the Shakespear Memorial National Theatre), was obviously marked out for selection; and it was generally expected that the Lords Lytton and Esher, who had taken a prominent part in the same movement, would have been added. This expectation was not fulfilled. Instead, Lord Willoughby de Broke, who had distinguished himself as an amateur actor, was selected along with Lord Newton, whose special qualifications for the Committee, if he had any, were unknown to the public. Finally Lord Ribblesdale, the argute son of a Scotch mother, was thrown in to make up for any shortcoming in intellectual subtlety that might arise in the case of his younger colleagues; and this completed the two teams.

THE COMMITTEE'S ATTITUDE TOWARDS THE THEATRE

In England, thanks chiefly to the censorship, the theatre is not respected. It is indulged and despised as a department of what is politely called gaiety. It is therefore not surprising that the majority of the Committee began by taking its work uppishly and carelessly. When it discovered that the contemporary drama, licensed by the Lord Chamberlain, included plays which could be described only behind closed doors, and in the discomfort which attends discussions of very nasty subjects between men of widely different ages, it calmly put its own convenience before its public duty by ruling that there should be no discussion of particular plays, much as if a committee on temperance were to rule that drunkenness was not a proper subject of conversation among gentlemen.

A BAD BEGINNING

This was a bad beginning. Everybody knew that in England the censorship would not be crushed by the weight of the constitutional argument against it, heavy as that was, unless it were also brought home to the Committee and to the public that it had sanctioned and protected the very worst practicable examples of the kind of play it professed to extirpate. For it must be remembered that the other half of the practical side of the case, dealing with the merits of the play it had suppressed, could never secure a unanimous assent. If the Censor had suppressed Hamlet, as he most certainly would have done had it been submitted to him as a new play, he would have been supported by a large body of people to whom incest is a tabooed subject which must not be mentioned on the stage or anywhere else outside a criminal court. Hamlet, Oedipus, and The Cenci, Mrs Warren's Profession, Brieux's Maternité, and Les Avariés, Maeterlinck's Monna Vanna and Mr Granville Barker's Waste may or may not be great poems, or edifying sermons, or important documents, or charming romances: our tribal citizens know nothing about that and do not want to know anything: all that they do know is that incest, prostitution, abortion, contagious diseases, and nudity are improper, and that all conversations, or books, or plays in which they are discussed are improper conversations, improper books, improper plays, and should not be allowed. The Censor may prohibit all such plays with complete certainty that there will be a chorus of 'Quite right too' sufficient to drown the protests of the few who know better. The Achilles heel of the censorship is therefore not the fine plays it has suppressed, but the abominable plays it has licensed: plays which the Committee itself had to turn the public out of the room and close the doors before it could discuss, and which I myself have found it impossible to expose in the press because no editor of a paper or magazine intended for general family reading could admit into his columns the baldest narration of the stories which the Censor has not only tolerated but expressly certified as fitting for presentation on the stage. When the Committee ruled out this part of the case it shook the confidence of the authors in its impartiality and its seriousness. Of course it was not able to enforce its ruling thoroughly. Plays which were merely lightminded and irresponsible in their viciousness were repeatedly mentioned by Mr Harcourt and others. But the really detestable plays, which would have damned the censorship beyond all apology or salvation, were never referred to; and the moment Mr Harcourt or anyone else made the Committee uncomfortable by a move in their direction, the ruling was appealed to at once, and the censorship saved.

A COMIC INTERLUDE

It was part of this nervous dislike of the unpleasant part of its business that led to the comic incident of the Committee's sudden discovery that I had insulted it, and its suspension of its investigation for the purpose of elaborately insulting me back again. Comic to the lookers-on, that is; for the majority of the Committee made no attempt to conceal the fact that they were wildly angry with me; and I, though my public experience and skill in acting enabled me to maintain an appearance of imperturbable good humor, was equally furious. The friction began as follows.

The precedents for the conduct of the Committee were to be found in the proceedings of the Committee of 1892. That Committee, no doubt recognizing the absurdity of calling on distinguished artists to give their views before it, and then refusing to allow them to state their views except in nervous replies to such questions as it might suit members to put to them, allowed Sir Henry Irving and Sir John Hare to prepare and read written statements, and formally invited them to read them to the Committee before being questioned. I accordingly prepared such a statement. For the greater convenience of the Committee, I offered to have this statement printed at my own expense, and to supply the members with copies. The offer was accepted; and the copies supplied. I also offered to provide the Committee with copies of those plays of mine which had been refused a licence by the Lord Chamberlain. That offer also was accepted; and the books duly supplied.

AN ANTI-SHAVIAN PANIC

As far as I can guess, the next thing that happened was that some timid or unawakened member of the Committee read my statement and was frightened or scandalized out of his wits by it. At all events it is certain that the majority of the Committee allowed themselves to be persuaded to refuse to allow any statement to be read; but to avoid the appearance of pointing this expressly at me, the form adopted was a resolution to adhere strictly to precedence, the Committee being then unaware that the precedents were on my side. Accordingly, when I appeared before the Committee, and proposed to read my statement 'according to the precedent,' the Committee was visibly taken aback. The Chairman was bound by the letter of the decision arrived at to allow me to read my statement, since that course was according to precedent; but as this was exactly what the decision was meant to prevent, the majority of the Committee would have regarded this hoisting of them with their own petard as a breach of faith on the part of the Chairman, who, I infer, was not in agreement with the suppressive majority. There was nothing for it, after a somewhat awkward pause, but to clear me and the public out of the room and reconsider the situation *in camera*. When the doors were opened again I was informed that the Committee would not hear my statement. But as the Committee could not very decently refuse my evidence altogether, the Chairman, with a printed copy of my statement in his hands as 'proof', was able to come to the rescue to some extent by putting to me a series of questions to which no doubt I might have replied by taking another copy out of my pocket, and quoting my statement paragraph by paragraph, as some of the later witnesses did. But as in offering the Committee my statement for burial in their bluebook I had made a considerable sacrifice, being able to secure greater publicity for it by independent publication on my own account; and as, further, the circumstances of the refusal made it offensive enough to take all heart out of the scrupulous consideration with which I had so far treated the Committee, I was not disposed to give its majority a second chance, or to lose the opportunity offered me by the questions to fire an additional broadside into the censorship. I pocketed my statement, and answered the questions *viva voce*. At the conclusion of this, my examination-in-chief, the Committee adjourned, asking me to present myself again for (virtually) cross-examination. But this cross-examination never came off, as the sequel will shew.

A RARE AND CURIOUS FIRST EDITION

The refusal of the Committee to admit my statement had not unnaturally created the impression that it must be a scandalous document; and a lively demand for copies at once set in. And among the very first applicants were members of the majority which had carried the decision to exclude the document. They had given so little attention to the business that they did not know, or had forgotten, that they had already been supplied with copies at their own request. At all events, they came to me publicly and cleaned me out of the handful of copies I had provided for distribution to the press. And after the sitting it was intimated to me that yet more copies were desired for the use of the Committee: a demand, under the circumstances, of breath-bereaving coolness. At the same time, a brisk demand arose outside the Committee, not only among people who were anxious to read what I had to say on the subject, but among victims of the craze for collecting first editions, copies of privately circulated pamphlets, and other real or imaginary rarities. Such maniacs will cheerfully pay five guineas for any piece of discarded old rubbish of mine when they will not pay as many shillings for a clean new copy of it, because everyone else can get it for the same price too.

THE TIMES TO THE RESCUE

The day after the refusal of the Committee to face my statement, I transferred the scene of action to the columns of The Times, which did yeoman's service to the public on this, as on many other occasions, by treating the question as a public one without the least regard to the supposed susceptibilities of the Court on the one side, or the avowed prejudices of the Free Churches or the interests of the managers or theatrical speculators on the other. The Times published the summarized conclusions of my statement, and gave me an opportunity of saying as much as it was then advisable to say of what had occurred. For it must be remembered that, however impatient and contemptuous I might feel of the intellectual cowardice shewn by the majority of the Committee face to face with myself, it was none the less necessary to keep up its prestige in every possible way, not only for the sake of the dignity and importance of the matter with which it had to deal and in the hope that the treatment of subsequent witnesses and the final report might make amends for a feeble beginning, but also out of respect and consideration for the minority. For it is fair to say that the majority was never more than a bare majority, and that the worst thing the Committee did – the exclusion of references to particular plays – was perpetrated in the absence of the Chairman.

I, therefore, had to treat the Committee in The Times very much better than its majority deserved, an injustice for which I now apologize. I did not, however, resist the temptation to hint, quite good-humoredly, that my politeness to the Committee had cost me quite enough already, and that I was not prepared to supply the members of the Committee, or anyone else, with extra copies merely as collectors' curiosities.

THE COUNCIL OF TEN

Then the fat was in the fire. The majority, chaffed for its eagerness to obtain copies of scarce pamphlets retailable at five guineas, went dancing mad. When I presented myself, as requested, for cross-examination, I found the doors of the Committee room shut, and the corridors of the House of Lords filled by a wondering crowd, to whom it had somehow leaked out that something terrible was happening inside. It could not be another licensed play too scandalous to be discussed in public, because the Committee had decided to discuss no more of these examples of the Censor's notions of purifying the stage; and what else the Committee might have to discuss that might not be heard by all the world was not easily guessable.

Without suggesting that the confidence of the Committee was in any way violated by any of its members further than was absolutely necessary to clear them from suspicion of complicity in the scene which followed, I think I may venture to conjecture what was happening. It was felt by the majority, first, that it must be cleared at all costs of the imputation of having procured more than one copy each of my statement, and that one not from any interest in an undesirable document by an irreverent author, but in the reluctant discharge of its solemn public duty; second, that a terrible example must be made of me by the most crashing public snub in the power of the Committee to administer. To throw my wretched little pamphlet at my head and to kick me out of the room was the passionate impulse which prevailed in spite of all the remonstrances of the Commoners, seasoned to the give-and-take of public life, and of the single peer who kept his head. The others, for the moment, had no heads to keep. And the fashion in which they proposed to wreak their vengeance was as follows.

THE SENTENCE

I was to be admitted, as a lamb to the slaughter, and allowed to take my place as if for further examination. The Chairman was then to inform me coldly that the Committee did not desire to have anything more to say to me. The members were thereupon solemnly to hand me back the copies of my statement as so much waste paper, and I was to be suffered to slink away with what countenance I could maintain in such disgrace.

But this plan required the active co-operation of every member of the Committee; and whilst the majority regarded it as an august and impressive vindication of the majesty of parliament, the minority regarded it with equal conviction as a puerile tomfoolery, and declined altogether to act their allotted parts in it. Besides, they did not all want to part with the books. For instance, Mr Hugh Law, being an Irishman, with an Irishman's sense of how to behave like a gallant gentleman on occasion, was determined to be able to assure me that nothing should induce him to give up my statement or prevent him from obtaining and cherishing as many copies as possible. (I quote this as an example to the House of Lords of the right thing to say in such emergencies.) So the program had to be modified. The minority could not prevent the enraged majority from refusing to examine me further; nor could the Chairman refuse to communicate that decision to me. Neither could the minority object to the secretary handing me back such copies as he could collect from the majority. And at that the matter was left. The doors were opened; the audience trooped in; I was called to my place in the dock (so to speak); and all was ready for the sacrifice.

THE EXECUTION

Alas! the majority reckoned without Colonel Lockwood. That hardy and undaunted veteran refused to shirk his share in the scene merely because the minority was recalcitrant and the majority perhaps subject to stage fright. When Mr Samuel had informed me that the Committee had no further questions to ask me with an urbanity which gave the public no clue as to the temper of the majority; when I had jumped up with the proper air of relief and gratitude; when the secretary had handed me his little packet of books with an affability which effectually concealed his dramatic function as executioner; when the audience was simply disappointed at being baulked of the entertainment of hearing Mr Robert Harcourt cross-examine me; in short, when the situation was all but saved by the tact of the Chairman and secretary, Colonel Lockwood rose, with all his carnations blazing, and gave away the whole case by handing me, with impressive simplicity and courtesy, his *two* copies of the precious statement. And I believe that if he had succeeded in securing ten, he would have handed them all back to me with the most sincere conviction that every one of the ten must prove a crushing addition to the weight of my discomfiture. I still cherish that second copy, a little blue-bound pamphlet, methodically autographed 'Lockwood B' among my most valued literary trophies.

An innocent lady told me afterwards that she never knew that I could smile so beautifully, and that she thought it shewed very good taste on my part. I was not conscious of smiling; but I should have embraced the Colonel had I dared. As it was, I turned expectantly to his colleagues, mutely inviting them to follow his example. But there was only one Colonel Lockwood on that Committee. No eye met mine except minority eyes, dancing with mischief. There was nothing more to be said. I went home to my morning's work, and returned in the afternoon to receive the apologies of the minority for the conduct of the majority, and to see Mr Granville Barker, overwhelmed by the conscience-stricken politeness of the now almost abject Committee, and by a powerful smell of carnations, heading the long list of playwrights who came there to testify against the censorship, and whose treatment, I am happy to say, was everything they could have desired.

After all, ridiculous as the scene was, Colonel Lockwood's simplicity and courage were much more serviceable to his colleagues than their own inept *coup de théâtre* would have been if he had not spoiled it. It was plain to everyone that he had acted in entire good faith, without a thought as to these apparently insignificant little books being of any importance or having caused me or anybody else any trouble, and that he was wounded in his most sensitive spot by the construction my Times letter had put on his action. And in Colonel Lockwood's case one saw the case of his party on the Committee. They had simply been thoughtless in the matter.

I hope nobody will suppose that this in any way exonerates them. When people accept public service for one of the most vital duties that can arise in our society, they have no right to be thoughtless. In spite of the fun of the scene on the surface, my public sense was, and still is, very deeply offended by it. It made an end for me of the claim of the majority to be taken seriously. When the Government comes to deal with the question, as it presumably will before long, I invite it to be guided by the Chairman, the minority, and by the witnesses according to their weight, and to pay no attention whatever to those recommendations which were obviously inserted solely to conciliate the majority and get the report through and the Committee done with.

My evidence will be found in the Bluebook, pp. 46–53. And here is the terrible statement which the Committee went through so much to suppress.

THE REJECTED STATEMENT – PART I

THE WITNESS'S QUALIFICATIONS

I am by profession a playwright. I have been in practice since 1892. I am a member of the Managing Sub-Committee of the Society of Authors and of the Dramatic Sub-Committee of that body. I have written nineteen plays, some of which have been translated and performed in all European countries except Turkey, Greece, and Portugal. They have been performed extensively in America. Three of them have been refused licences by the Lord Chamberlain. In one case a licence has since been granted. The other two are still unlicensed. I have suffered both in pocket and reputation by the action of the Lord Chamberlain. In other countries I have not come into conflict with the censorship except in Austria, where the production of a comedy of mine was postponed for a year because it alluded to the part taken by Austria in the Servo-Bulgarian war. This comedy was not one of the plays suppressed in England by the Lord Chamberlain. One of the plays so suppressed was prosecuted in America by the police in consequence of an immense crowd of disorderly persons having been attracted to the first performance by the Lord Chamberlain's condemnation of it; but on appeal to a higher court it was decided that the representation was lawful and the intention innocent, since when it has been repeatedly performed.

I am not an ordinary playwright in general practice. I am a specialist in immoral and heretical plays. My reputation has been gained by my persistent struggle to force the public to reconsider its morals. In particular, I regard much current morality as to economic and sexual relations as disastrously wrong; and I regard certain doctrines of the Christian religion as understood in England today with abhorrence. I write plays with the deliberate object of converting the nation to my opinions in these matters. I have no other effectual incentive to write plays, as I am not dependent on the theatre for my livelihood. If I were prevented from producing immoral and heretical plays, I should cease to write for the theatre, and propagate my views from the platform and through books. I mention these facts to shew that I have a special interest in the achievement by my profession of those rights of liberty of speech and conscience which are matters of course in other professions. I object to censorship not merely because the existing form of it grievously injures and hinders me individually, but on public grounds.

THE DEFINITION OF IMMORALITY

In dealing with the question of the censorship, everything depends on the correct use of the word immorality, and a careful discrimination between the powers of a magistrate or judge to administer a code, and those of a censor to please himself.

Whatever is contrary to established manners and customs is

immoral. An immoral act or doctrine is not necessarily a sinful one: on the contrary, every advance in thought and conduct is by definition immoral until it has converted the majority. For this reason it is of the most enormous importance that immorality should be protected jealously against the attacks of those who have no standard except the standard of custom, and who regard any attack on custom – that is, on morals – as an attack on society, on religion, and on virtue.

A censor is never intentionally a protector of immorality. He always aims at the protection of morality. Now morality is extremely valuable to society. It imposes conventional conduct on the great mass of persons who are incapable of original ethical judgment, and who would be quite lost if they were not in leading-strings devised by lawgivers, philosophers, prophets, and poets for their guidance. But morality is not dependent on censorship for protection. It is already powerfully fortified by the magistracy and the whole body of law. Blasphemy, indecency, libel, treason, sedition, obscenity, profanity, and all the other evils which a censorship is supposed to avert, are punishable by the civil magistrate with all the severity of vehement prejudice. Morality has not only every engine that lawgivers can devise in full operation for its protection, but also that enormous weight of public opinion enforced by social ostracism which is stronger than all the statutes. A censor pretending to protect morality is like a child pushing the cushions of a railway carriage to give itself the sensation of making the train travel at sixty miles an hour. It is immorality, not morality, that needs protection: it is morality, not immorality, that needs restraint; for morality, with all the dead weight of human inertia and superstition to hang on the back of the pioneer, and all the malice of vulgarity and prejudice to threaten him, is responsible for many persecutions and many martyrdoms.

Persecutions and martyrdoms, however, are trifles compared to the mischief done by censorships in delaying the general march of enlightenment. This can be brought home to us by imagining what would have been the effect of applying to all literature the censorship we still apply to the stage. The works of Linnaeus and the evolutionists of 1790–1830, of Darwin, Wallace, Huxley, Helmholtz, Tyndall, Spencer, Carlyle, Ruskin, and Samuel Butler, would not have been published, as they were all immoral and heretical in the very highest degree, and gave pain to many worthy and pious people. They are at present condemned by the Greek and Roman Catholic censorships as unfit for general reading. A censorship of conduct would have been equally disastrous. The disloyalty of Hampden and of Washington; the revolting immorality of Luther in not only marrying when he was a priest, but actually marrying a nun; the heterodoxy of Galileo; the shocking blasphemies and sacrileges of Mahomet against the idols whom he dethroned to make way for his conception of one god; the still more startling blasphemy of Jesus when He declared God to be the son of man and Himself to be the son of God, are all examples of shocking immoralities (every immorality shocks somebody), the suppression and extinction of which would have been more disastrous than the utmost mischief that can be conceived as ensuing from the toleration of vice.

These facts, glaring as they are, are disguised by the promotion of immoralities into moralities which is constantly going on. Christianity and Mahometanism, once thought of and dealt with exactly as Anarchism is thought of and dealt with today, have become established religions; and fresh immoralities are persecuted in their name. The truth is that the vast majority of persons professing these religions have never been anything but simple moralists. The respectable Englishman who is a Christian because he was born in Clapham would be a Mahometan for the cognate reason if he had been born in Constantinople. He has never willingly tolerated immorality. He did not adopt any innovation until it had become moral; and then he adopted it, not on its merits, but solely because it had become moral. In doing so he never realized that it had ever been immoral: consequently its early struggles taught him no lesson; and he has opposed the next step in human progress as indignantly as if neither manners, customs, nor thought had ever changed since the beginning of the world. Toleration must be imposed on him as a mystic and painful duty by his spiritual and political leaders, or he will condemn the world to stagnation, which is the penalty of an inflexible morality.

WHAT TOLERATION MEANS

This must be done all the more arbitrarily because it is not possible to make the ordinary moral man understand what toleration and liberty really mean. He will accept them verbally with alacrity, even with enthusiasm, because the word toleration has been moralized by eminent Whigs; but what he means by toleration is toleration of doctrines that he considers enlightened, and, by liberty, liberty to do what he considers right: that is, he does not mean toleration or liberty at all; for there is no need to tolerate what appears enlightened or to claim liberty to do what most people consider right. Toleration and liberty have no sense or use except as toleration of opinions that are considered damnable, and liberty to do what seems wrong. Setting Englishmen free to marry their deceased wife's sisters is not tolerated by the people who approve of it, but by the people who regard it as incestuous. Catholic Emancipation and the admission of Jews to parliament needed no toleration from Catholics and Jews: the toleration they needed was that of the people who regarded the one measure as a facilitation of idolatry, and the other as a condonation of the crucifixion. Clearly such toleration is not clamored for by the multitude or by the press which reflects its prejudices. It is essentially one of those abnegations of passion and prejudice which the common man submits to because uncommon men whom he respects as wiser than himself assure him that it must be so, or the higher affairs of human destiny will suffer.

Such submission is the more difficult because the arguments against tolerating immorality are the same as the arguments against tolerating murder and theft; and this is why the Censor seems to the inconsiderate as obviously desirable a functionary as the police magistrate. But there is this simple and tremendous difference between the cases: that whereas no evil can conceivably result from the total suppression of murder and theft, and all communities prosper in direct proportion to such suppression, the total suppression of immorality, especially in matters of religion and sex, would stop enlightenment, and produce what used to be called a Chinese civilization until the Chinese lately took to immoral courses by permitting railway contractors to desecrate the graves of their ancestors, and their soldiers to wear clothes which indecently revealed the fact that they had legs and waists and even posteriors. At about the same moment a few bold Englishwomen ventured on the immorality of riding astride their horses, a practice that has since established itself so successfully that before another generation has passed away there may not be a new side-saddle in England, or a woman who could use it if there was.

THE CASE FOR TOLERATION

Accordingly, there has risen among wise and far-sighted men a perception of the need for setting certain departments of human activity entirely free from legal interference. This has nothing to do with any sympathy those liberators may themselves have with immoral views. A man with the strongest conviction of the Divine ordering of the universe and of the superiority of monarchy to all forms of government may nevertheless quite consistently and conscientiously be ready to lay down his life for the right of every man to advocate Atheism or Republicanism if he believes in them. An attack on morals may turn out to be the salvation of the race. A hundred years ago nobody foresaw that Tom Paine's centenary would be the subject of a laudatory special article in The Times; and only a few understood that the persecution of his works and the transportation of men for the felony of reading them was a mischievous mistake. Even less, perhaps, could they have guessed that Proudhon, who became notorious by his essay entitled 'What is Property? It is Theft,' would have received, on the like occasion and in the same paper, a respectful consideration which nobody would dream now of according to Lord Liverpool or Lord Brougham. Nevertheless there was a mass of evidence to shew that such a development was not only possible but fairly probable, and that the risks of suppressing liberty of propaganda were far graver than the risk of Paine's or Proudhon's writings wrecking civilization. Now there was no such evidence in favor of tolerating the cutting of throats and the robbing of tills. No case whatever can be made out for the statement that a nation cannot do without common thieves and homicidal ruffians. But an overwhelming case can be made out for the statement that no nation can prosper or even continue to exist without heretics and advocates of shockingly immoral doctrines. The Inquisition and the Star Chamber, which were nothing but censorships, made ruthless war on impiety and immorality. The result was once familiar to Englishmen, though of late years it seems to have been forgotten. It cost England a revolution to get rid of the Star Chamber. Spain did not get rid of the Inquisition, and paid for that omission by becoming a barely third-rate power politically, and intellectually no power at all, in the Europe she had once dominated as the mightiest of the Christian empires.

THE LIMITS TO TOLERATION

But the large toleration these considerations dictate has limits. For example, though we tolerate, and rightly tolerate, the propaganda of Anarchism as a political theory which embraces all that is valuable in the doctrine of Laisser-Faire and the method of Free Trade as well as all that is shocking in the views of Bakounine, we clearly cannot, or at all events will not, tolerate assassination of rulers on the ground that it is 'propaganda by deed' or sociological experiment. A play inciting to such an assassination cannot claim the privileges of heresy or immorality, because no case can be made out in support of assassination as an indispensable instrument of progress. Now it happens that we have in the Julius Cæsar of Shakespear a play which the Tsar of Russia or the Governor-General of India would hardly care to see performed in their capitals just now. It is an artistic treasure; but it glorifies a murder which Goethe described as the silliest crime ever committed. It may quite possibly have helped the regicides of 1649 to see themselves, as it certainly helped generations of Whig statesmen to see them, in a heroic light; and it unquestionably vindicates and ennobles a conspirator who assassinated the head of the Roman State not because he abused his position but solely because he occupied it, thus affirming the extreme republican principle that all kings, good or bad, should be killed because kingship and freedom cannot live together. Under certain circumstances this vindication and ennoblement might act as an incitement to an actual assassination as well as to Plutarchian republicanism; for it is one thing to advocate republicanism or royalism: it is quite another to make a hero of Brutus or Ravaillac, or a heroine of Charlotte Corday. Assassination is the extreme form of censorship; and it seems hard to justify an incitement to it on anti-censorial principles. The very people who would have scouted the notion of prohibiting the performances of Julius Cæsar at His Majesty's Theatre in London last year, might now entertain very seriously a proposal to exclude Indians from them, and to suppress the play completely in Calcutta and Dublin; for if the assassin of Cæsar was a hero, why not the assassins of Lord Frederick Cavendish, Presidents Lincoln and McKinley, and Sir Curzon Wyllie? Here is a strong case for some constitutional means of preventing the performance of a play. True, it is an equally strong case for preventing the circulation of the Bible, which was always in the hands of our regicides; but as the Roman Catholic Church does not hesitate to accept that consequence of the censorial principle, it does not invalidate the argument.

Take another actual case. A modern comedy, Arms and The Man, though not a comedy of politics, is nevertheless so far historical that it reveals the unacknowledged fact that as the Servo-Bulgarian War of 1885 was much more than a struggle between the Servians and Bulgarians, the troops engaged were officered by two European Powers of the first magnitude. In consequence, the performance of the play was for some time forbidden in Vienna, and more recently it gave offence in Rome at a moment when popular feeling was excited as to the relations of Austria with the Balkan States. Now if a comedy so remote from political passion as Arms and The Man can, merely because it refers to political facts, become so inconvenient and inopportune that Foreign Offices take the trouble to have its production postponed, what may not be the effect of what is called a patriotic drama produced at a moment when the balance is quivering between peace and war? Is there not something to be said for a political censorship, if not for a moral one? May not those continental governments who leave the stage practically free in every other respect, but muzzle it politically, be justified by the practical exigencies of the situation?

THE DIFFERENCE BETWEEN LAW AND CENSORSHIP

The answer is that a pamphlet, a newspaper article, or a resolution moved at a political meeting can do all the mischief that a play can, and often more; yet we do not set up a permanent censorship of the press or of political meetings. Any journalist may publish an article, any demagogue may deliver a speech without giving notice to the government or obtaining its licence. The risk of such freedom is great; but as it is the price of our political liberty, we think it worth paying. We may abrogate it in emergencies by a Coercion Act, a suspension of the Habeas Corpus Act, or a proclamation of martial law, just as we stop the traffic in a street during a fire, or shoot thieves at sight if they loot after an earthquake. But when the emergency is past, liberty is restored everywhere except in the theatre. The Act of 1843 is a permanent Coercion Act for the theatre, a permanent suspension of the Habeas Corpus Act as far as plays are concerned, a permanent proclamation of martial law with a single official substituted for a court martial. It is, in fact, assumed that actors, playwrights, and theatre managers are dangerous and dissolute characters whose existence creates a chronic state of emergency, and who must be treated as earthquake looters are treated. It is not necessary now to discredit this assumption. It was broken down by the late Sir Henry Irving when he finally shamed the Government into extending to his profession the official recognition enjoyed by the other branches of fine art. Today we have on the roll of knighthood actors, authors, and managers. The rogue and vagabond theory of the depravity of the theatre is as dead officially as it is in general society; and with it has perished the sole excuse for the Act of 1843 and for the denial to the theatre of the liberties secured, at far greater social risk, to the press and the platform.

There is no question here of giving the theatre any larger liberties than the press and the platform, or of claiming larger powers for Shakespear to eulogize Brutus than Lord Rosebery has to eulogize Cromwell. The abolition of the censorship does not involve the abolition of the magistrate and of the whole civil and criminal code. On the contrary, it would make the theatre more effectually subject to them than it is at present; for once a play now runs the gauntlet of the censorship, it is practically placed above the law. It is almost humiliating to have to demonstrate the essential difference between a censor and a magistrate or a sanitary inspector; but it is impossible to ignore the carelessness with which even distinguished critics of the theatre assume that all the arguments proper to the support of a magistracy and body of jurisprudence apply equally to a censorship.

A magistrate has laws to administer: a censor has nothing but his own opinion. A judge leaves the question of guilt to the jury: the Censor is jury and judge as well as lawgiver. A magistrate may be strongly prejudiced against an atheist or an anti-vaccinator, just as the sanitary inspector may have formed a careful opinion that drains are less healthy than cesspools; but the magistrate must allow the atheist to affirm instead of to swear, and must grant the anti-vaccinator an exemption certificate, when their demands are lawfully made; and in cities the inspector must compel the builder to make drains and must prosecute him if he makes cesspools. The law may be only the intolerance of the community; but it is a defined and limited intolerance. The limitation is sometimes carried so far that a judge cannot inflict the penalty for housebreaking on a burglar who can prove that he found the door open and therefore made only an unlawful entry. On the other hand, it is sometimes so vague, as for example in the case of the American law against obscenity, that it makes the magistrate virtually a censor. But in the main a citizen can ascertain what he may do and what he may not do; and, though no one knows better than a magistrate that a single ill-conducted family may demoralize a whole street, no magistrate can imprison or otherwise restrain its members on the ground that their immorality may corrupt their neighbors. He can prevent any citizen from carrying certain specified weapons, but not from handling pokers, table-knives, bricks or bottles of corrosive fluid, on the ground that he might use them to commit murder or inflict malicious injury. He has no general power to prevent citizens from selling unhealthy or poisonous substances, or judging for themselves what substances are unhealthy and what wholesome, what poisonous and what innocuous: what he *can* do is to prevent anybody who has not a specific qualification from selling certain specified poisons of which a schedule is kept. Nobody is forbidden to sell minerals without a licence; but everybody is forbidden to sell silver without a licence. When the law has forgotten some atrocious sin – for instance, contracting marriage whilst suffering from contagious disease – the magistrate cannot arrest or punish the wrongdoer, however he may abhor his wickedness. In short, no man is lawfully at the mercy of the magistrate's personal caprice, prejudice, ignorance, superstition, temper, stupidity, resentment, timidity, ambition, or private conviction. But a playwright's livelihood, his reputation, and his inspiration and mission are at the personal mercy of the Censor. The two do not stand, as the criminal and the judge stand, in the presence of a law that binds them both equally, and was made by neither of them, but by the deliberate collective wisdom of the community. The only law that affects them is the Act of 1843, which empowers one of them to do absolutely and finally what he likes with the other's work. And when it is remembered that the slave in this case is the man whose profession is that of Eschylus and Euripides, of Shakespear and Goethe, of Tolstoy and Ibsen, and the master the holder of a party appointment which by the nature of its duties practically excludes the possibility of its acceptance by a serious statesman or great lawyer, it will be seen that the playwrights are justified in reproaching the framers of that Act for having failed not only to appreciate the immense importance of the theatre as a most powerful instrument for teaching the nation how and what to think and feel, but even to conceive that those who make their living by the theatre are normal human beings with the common rights of English citizens. In this extremity of inconsiderateness it is not surprising that they also did not trouble themselves to study the difference between a censor and a magistrate. And it will be found that almost all the people who disinterestedly defend the censorship today are defending him on the assumption that there is no constitutional difference between him and any other functionary whose duty it is to restrain crime and disorder.

One further difference remains to be noted. As a magistrate

grows old his mind may change or decay; but the law remains the same. The censorship of the theatre fluctuates with every change in the views and character of the man who exercises it. And what this implies can only be appreciated by those who can imagine what the effect on the mind must be of the duty of reading through every play that is produced in the kingdom year in, year out.

WHY THE LORD CHAMBERLAIN?

What may be called the high political case against censorship as a principle is now complete. The pleadings are those which have already freed books and pulpits and political platforms in England from censorship, if not from occasional legal persecution. The stage alone remains under a censorship of a grotesquely unsuitable kind. No play can be performed if the Lord Chamberlain happens to disapprove of it. And the Lord Chamberlain's functions have no sort of relationship to dramatic literature. A great judge of literature, a far-seeing statesman, a born champion of liberty of conscience and intellectual integrity – say a Milton, a Chesterfield, a Bentham – would be a very bad Lord Chamberlain: so bad, in fact, that his exclusion from such a post may be regarded as decreed by natural law. On the other hand, a good Lord Chamberlain would be a stickler for morals in the narrowest sense, a busy-body, a man to whom a matter of two inches in the length of a gentleman's sword or the absence of a feather from a lady's head-dress would be a graver matter than the Habeas Corpus Act. The Lord Chamberlain, as Censor of the theatre, is a direct descendant of the King's Master of the Revels, appointed in 1544 by Henry VIII to keep order among the players and musicians of that day when they performed at Court. This first appearance of the theatrical censor in politics as the whipper-in of the player, with its conception of the player as a rich man's servant hired to amuse him, and, outside his professional duties, as a gay, disorderly, anarchic spoilt child, half privileged, half outlawed, probably as much vagabond as actor, is the real foundation of the subjection of the whole profession, actors, managers, authors and all, to the despotic authority of an officer whose business it is to preserve decorum among menials. It must be remembered that it was not until a hundred years later, in the reaction against the Puritans, that a woman could appear on the English stage without being pelted off as the Italian actresses were. The theatrical profession was regarded as a shameless one; and it is only of late years that actresses have at last succeeded in living down the assumption that actress and prostitute are synonymous terms, and made good their position in respectable society. This makes the survival of the old ostracism in the Act of 1843 intolerably galling; and though it explains the apparently unaccountable absurdity of choosing as Censor of dramatic literature an official whose functions and qualifications have nothing whatever to do with literature, it also explains why the present arrangement is not only criticized as an institution, but resented as an insult.

THE DIPLOMATIC OBJECTION TO THE LORD CHAMBERLAIN

There is another reason, quite unconnected with the susceptibilities of authors, which makes it undesirable that a member of the King's Household should be responsible for the character and tendency of plays. The drama, dealing with all departments of human life, is necessarily political. Recent events have shewn – what indeed needed no demonstration – that it is impossible to prevent inferences being made, both at home and abroad, from the action of the Lord Chamberlain. The most talked-about play of the present year (1909), An Englishman's Home, has for its main interest an invasion of England by a fictitious power which is understood, as it is meant to be understood, to represent Germany. The lesson taught by the play is the danger of invasion and the need for every English citizen to be a soldier. The Lord Chamberlain licensed this play, but refused to license a parody of it. Shortly afterwards he refused to license another play in which the fear of a German invasion was ridiculed. The German press drew the inevitable inference that the Lord Chamberlain was an anti-German alarmist, and that his opinions were a reflection of those prevailing in St James's Palace. Immediately after this, the Lord

Chamberlain licensed the play. Whether the inference, as far as the Lord Chamberlain was concerned, was justified, is of no consequence. What is important is that it was sure to be made, justly or unjustly, and extended from the Lord Chamberlain to the Throne.

THE OBJECTION OF COURT ETIQUET

There is another objection to the Lord Chamberlain's censorship which affects the author's choice of subject. Formerly very little heed was given in England to the susceptibilities of foreign courts. For instance, the notion that the Mikado of Japan should be as sacred to the English playwright as he is to the Japanese Lord Chamberlain would have seemed grotesque a generation ago. Now that the maintenance of *entente cordiale* between nations is one of the most prominent and most useful functions of the crown, the freedom of authors to deal with political subjects, even historically, is seriously threatened by the way in which the censorship makes the King responsible for the contents of every play. One author – the writer of these lines, in fact – has long desired to dramatize the life of Mahomet. But the possibility of a protest from the Turkish Ambassador – or the fear of it – causing the Lord Chamberlain to refuse to license such a play has prevented the play from being written. Now, if the censorship were abolished, nobody but the author could be held responsible for the play. The Turkish Ambassador does not now protest against the publication of Carlyle's essay on the prophet, or of the English translations of the Koran in the prefaces to which Mahomet is criticized as an impostor, or of the older books in which he is reviled as Mahound and classed with the devil himself. But if these publications had to be licensed by the Lord Chamberlain it would be impossible for the King to allow the licence to be issued, as he would thereby be made responsible for the opinions expressed. This restriction of the historical drama is an unmixed evil. Great religious leaders are more interesting and more important subjects for the dramatist than great conquerors. It is a misfortune that public opinion would not tolerate a dramatization of Mahomet in Constantinople. But to prohibit it here, where public opinion would tolerate it, is an absurdity which, if applied in all directions, would make it impossible for the Queen to receive a Turkish ambassador without veiling herself, or the Dean and Chapter of St Paul's to display a cross on the summit of their Cathedral in a city occupied largely and influentially by Jews. Court etiquet is no doubt an excellent thing for court ceremonies; but to attempt to impose it on the drama is about as sensible as an attempt to make everybody in London wear court dress.

WHY NOT AN ENLIGHTENED CENSORSHIP?

In the above cases the general question of censorship is separable from the question of the present form of it. Everyone who condemns the principle of censorship must also condemn the Lord Chamberlain's control of the drama; but those who approve of the principle do not necessarily approve of the Lord Chamberlain being the Censor *ex officio*. They may, however, be entirely opposed to popular liberties, and may conclude from what has been said, not that the stage should be made as free as the church, press, or platform, but that these institutions should be censored as strictly as the stage. It will seem obvious to them that nothing is needed to remove all objections to a censorship except the placing of its powers in better hands.

Now though the transfer of the censorship to, say, the Lord Chancellor, or the Primate, or a Cabinet Minister, would be much less humiliating to the persons immediately concerned, the inherent vices of the institution would not be appreciably less disastrous. They would even be aggravated, for reasons which do not appear on the surface, and therefore need to be followed with some attention.

It is often said that the public is the real censor. That this is to some extent true is proved by the fact that plays which are licensed and produced in London have to be expurgated for the provinces. This does not mean that the provinces are more strait-laced, but simply that in many provincial towns there is only one theatre for all classes and all tastes, whereas in London there are separate theatres for separate sections of playgoers: so that, for example, Sir

Herbert Beerbohm Tree can conduct His Majesty's Theatre without the slightest regard to the tastes of the frequenters of the Gaiety Theatre; and Mr George Edwardes can conduct the Gaiety Theatre without catering in any way for lovers of Shakespear. Thus the farcical comedy which has scandalized the critics in London by the libertinage of its jests is played to the respectable dress circle of Northampton with these same jests slurred over so as to be imperceptible by even the most prurient spectator. The public, in short, takes care that nobody shall outrage it.

But the public also takes care that nobody shall starve it, or regulate its dramatic diet as a schoolmistress regulates the reading of her pupils. Even when it wishes to be debauched, no censor can – or at least no censor does – stand out against it. If a play is irresistibly amusing, it gets licensed no matter what its moral aspect may be. A brilliant instance is the Divorçons of the late Victorien Sardou, which may not have been the naughtiest play of the 19th century, but was certainly the very naughtiest that any English manager in his senses would have ventured to produce. Nevertheless, being a very amusing play, it passed the licenser with the exception of a reference to impotence as a ground for divorce which no English actress would have ventured on in any case. Within the last few months a very amusing comedy with a strongly polygamous moral was found irresistible by the Lord Chamberlain. Plenty of fun and a happy ending will get anything licensed, because the public will have it so, and the Examiner of Plays, as the holder of the office testified before the Commission of 1892 (Report, page 330), feels with the public, and knows that his office could not survive a widespread unpopularity. In short, the support of the mob – that is, of the unreasoning, unorganized, uninstructed mass of popular sentiment – is indispensable to the censorship as it exists today in England. This is the explanation of the toleration by the Lord Chamberlain of coarse and vicious plays. It is not long since a judge before whom a licensed play came in the course of a lawsuit expressed his scandalized astonishment at the licensing of such a work. Eminent churchmen have made similar protests. In some plays the simulation of criminal assaults on the stage has been carried to a point at which a step further would have involved the interference of the police. Provided the treatment of the theme is gaily or hypocritically popular, and the ending happy, the indulgence of the Lord Chamberlain can be counted on. On the other hand, anything unpleasing and unpopular is rigorously censored. Adultery and prostitution are tolerated and even encouraged to such an extent that plays which do not deal with them are commonly said not to be plays at all. But if any of the unpleasing consequences of adultery and prostitution – for instance, an *unsuccessful* illegal operation (successful ones are tolerated) or venereal disease – are mentioned, the play is prohibited. This principle of shielding the playgoer from unpleasant reflections is carried so far that when a play was submitted for licence in which the relations of a prostitute with all the male characters in the piece was described as 'immoral', the Examiner of Plays objected to that passage, though he made no objection to the relations themselves. The Lord Chamberlain dare not, in short, attempt to exclude from the stage the tragedies of murder and lust, or the farces of mendacity, adultery, and dissolute gaiety in which vulgar people delight. But when these same vulgar people are threatened with any unpopular play in which dissoluteness is shewn to be no laughing matter, it is prohibited at once amid the vulgar applause, the net result being that vice is made delightful and virtue banned by the very institution which is supported on the understanding that it produces exactly the opposite result.

THE WEAKNESS OF THE LORD CHAMBERLAIN'S DEPARTMENT

Now comes the question, Why is our censorship, armed as it is with apparently autocratic powers, so scandalously timid in the face of the mob? Why is it not as autocratic in dealing with playwrights below the average as with those above it? The answer is that its position is really a very weak one. It has no direct coercive forces, no funds to institute prosecutions and recover the legal penalties of defying it, no powers of arrest or imprisonment, in short, none of the guarantees of autocracy. What it can do is to refuse to renew the licence of a theatre at which its orders are disobeyed. When it happens that a theatre is about to be demolished, as was the case recently with the Imperial Theatre after it had passed into the hands of the Wesleyan Methodists, unlicensed plays can be performed, technically in private, but really in full publicity, without risk. The prohibited plays of Brieux and Ibsen have been performed in London in this way with complete impunity. But the impunity is not confined to condemned theatres. Not long ago a West End manager allowed a prohibited play to be performed at his theatre, taking his chance of losing his licence in consequence. The event proved that the manager was justified in regarding the risk as negligible; for the Lord Chamberlain's remedy – the closing of a popular and well-conducted theatre – was far too extreme to be practicable. Unless the play had so outraged public opinion as to make the manager odious and provoke a clamor for his exemplary punishment, the Lord Chamberlain could only have had his revenge at the risk of having his powers abolished as unsupportably tyrannical.

The Lord Chamberlain then has his powers so adjusted that he is tyrannical just where it is important that he should be tolerant, and tolerant just where he could screw up the standard a little by being tyrannical. His plea that there are unmentionable depths to which managers and authors would descend if he did not prevent them is disproved by the plain fact that his indulgence goes as far as the police, and sometimes further than the public, will let it. If our judges had so little power there would be no law in England. If our churches had so much, there would be no theatre, no literature, no science, no art, possibly no England. The institution is at once absurdly despotic and abjectly weak.

AN ENLIGHTENED CENSORSHIP STILL WORSE THAN THE LORD CHAMBERLAIN'S

Clearly a censorship of judges, bishops, or statesmen would not be in this abject condition. It would no doubt make short work of the coarse and vicious pieces which now enjoy the protection of the Lord Chamberlain, or at least of those of them in which the vulgarity and vice are discoverable by merely reading the prompt copy. But it would certainly disappoint the main hope of its advocates: the hope that it would protect and foster the higher drama. It would do nothing of the sort. On the contrary, it would inevitably suppress it more completely than the Lord Chamberlain does, because it would understand it better. The one play of Ibsen's which is prohibited on the English stage, Ghosts, is far less subversive than A Doll's House. But the Lord Chamberlain does not meddle with such far-reaching matters as the tendency of a play. He refuses to license Ghosts exactly as he would refuse to license Hamlet if it were submitted to him as a new play. He would license even Hamlet if certain alterations were made in it. He would disallow the incestuous relationship between the King and Queen. He would probably insist on the substitution of some fictitious country for Denmark in deference to the near relations of our reigning house with that realm. He would certainly make it an absolute condition that the closet scene, in which a son, in an agony of shame and revulsion, reproaches his mother for her relations with his uncle, should be struck out as unbearably horrifying and improper. But compliance with these conditions would satisfy him. He would raise no speculative objections to the tendency of the play.

This indifference to the larger issues of a theatrical performance could not be safely predicated of an enlightened censorship. Such a censorship might be more liberal in its toleration of matters which are only objected to on the ground that they are not usually discussed in general social conversation or in the presence of children; but it would presumably have a far deeper insight to and concern for the real ethical tendency of the play. For instance, had it been in existence during the last quarter of a century, it would have perceived that those plays of Ibsen's which have been licensed without question are fundamentally immoral to an altogether extraordinary degree. Every one of them is a deliberate act of war on society as at present constituted. Religion, marriage, ordinary respectability, are subjected to a destructive exposure and criticism which seems to mere moralists – that is, to persons of no more than average depth of mind – to be diabolical. It is no exaggeration to say that Ibsen gained his overwhelming reputation by undertaking a task of no less magnitude than changing the mind of Europe with the view of changing its morals. Now you cannot license work of that sort without making yourself responsible for it. The Lord Chamberlain accepted the responsibility because he did not understand it or concern himself about it. But what really enlightened and conscientious official dare take such a responsibility? The strength of character and range of vision which made Ibsen capable of it are not to be expected from any official, however eminent. It is true that an enlightened censor might, whilst shrinking even with horror from Ibsen's views, perceive that any nation which suppressed Ibsen would presently find itself falling behind the nations which tolerated him just as Spain fell behind England; but the proper action to take on such a conviction is the abdication of censorship, not the practice of it. As long as a censor is a censor, he cannot endorse by his licence opinions which seem to him dangerously heretical.

We may, therefore, conclude that the more enlightened a censorship is, the worse it would serve us. The Lord Chamberlain, an obviously unenlightened Censor, prohibits Ghosts and licenses all the rest of Ibsen's plays. An enlightened censorship would possibly license Ghosts; but it would certainly suppress many of the other plays. It would suppress subversiveness as well as what is called bad taste. The Lord Chamberlain prohibits one play by Sophocles because, like Hamlet, it mentions the subject of incest; but an enlightened censorship might suppress all the plays of Euripides because Euripides, like Ibsen, was a revolutionary Freethinker. Under the Lord Chamberlain, we can smuggle a good deal of immoral drama and almost as much coarsely vulgar and furtively lascivious drama as we like. Under a college of cardinals, or bishops, or judges, or any other conceivable form of experts in morals, philosophy, religion, or politics, we should get little except stagnant mediocrity.

THE PRACTICAL IMPOSSIBILITIES OF CENSORSHIP

There is, besides, a crushing material difficulty in the way of an enlightened censorship. It is not too much to say that the work involved would drive a man of any intellectual rank mad. Consider, for example, the Christmas pantomimes. Imagine a judge of the High Court, or an archbishop, or a Cabinet Minister, or an eminent man of letters, earning his living by reading through the mass of trivial doggerel represented by all the pantomimes which are put into rehearsal simultaneously at the end of every year. The proposal to put such mind-destroying drudgery upon an official of the class implied by the demand for an enlightened censorship falls through the moment we realize what it implies in practice.

Another material difficulty is that no play can be judged by merely reading the dialogue. To be fully effective a censor should witness the performance. The *mise-en-scène* of a play is as much a part of it as the words spoken on the stage. No censor could possibly object to such a speech as 'Might I speak to you for a moment, miss?' yet that apparently innocent phrase has often been made offensively improper on the stage by popular low comedians, with the effect of changing the whole character and meaning of the play as understood by the official Examiner. In one of the plays of the present season, the dialogue was that of a crude melodrama dealing in the most conventionally correct manner with the fortunes of a good-hearted and virtuous girl. Its morality was that of the Sunday school. But the principal actress, between two speeches which contained no reference to her action, changed her underclothing on the stage! It is true that in this case the actress was so much better than her part that she succeeded in turning what was meant as an impropriety into an inoffensive stroke of realism; yet it is none the less clear that stage business of this character, on which there can be no check except the actual presence of a censor in the theatre, might convert any dialogue, however innocent, into just the sort of entertainment against which the Censor is supposed to protect the public.

It was this practical impossibility that prevented the London County Council from attempting to apply a censorship of the Lord Chamberlain's pattern to the London music halls. A proposal to examine all entertainments before permitting their performance was actually made; and it was abandoned, not in the least as contrary to the liberty of the stage, but because the executive problem of how to do it at once reduced the proposal to absurdity. Even if the Council devoted all its time to witnessing rehearsals of variety performance, and putting each item to the vote, possibly after a prolonged discussion followed by a division, the work would still fall into arrear. No committee could be induced to undertake such a task. The attachment of an inspector of morals to each music hall would have meant an appreciable addition to the ratepayers' burden. In the face of such difficulties the proposal melted away. Had it been pushed through, and the inspectors appointed, each of them would have become a censor, and the whole body of inspectors would have become a *police des mœurs*. Those who know the history of such police forces on the Continent will understand how impossible it would be to procure inspectors whose characters would stand the strain of their opportunities of corruption, both pecuniary and personal, at such salaries as a local authority could be persuaded to offer.

It has been suggested that the present censorship should be supplemented by a board of experts, who should deal, not with the whole mass of plays sent up for licence, but only those which the Examiner of Plays refuses to pass. As the number of plays which the Examiner refuses to pass is never great enough to occupy a Board in permanent session with regular salaries, and as casual employment is not compatible with public responsibility, this proposal would work out in practice as an addition to the duties of some existing functionary. A Secretary of State would be objectionable as likely to be biased politically. An ecclesiastical referee might be biased against the theatre altogether. A judge in chambers would be the proper authority. This plan would combine the inevitable intolerance of an enlightened censorship with the popular laxity of the Lord Chamberlain. The judge would suppress the pioneers, whilst the Examiner of Plays issued two guinea certificates for the vulgar and vicious plays. For this reason the plan would no doubt be popular; but it would be very much as a relaxation of the administration of the Public Health Acts accompanied by the cheapening of gin would be popular.

THE ARBITRATION PROPOSAL

On the occasion of a recent deputation of playwrights to the Prime Minister it was suggested that if a censorship be inevitable, provision should be made for an appeal from the Lord Chamberlain in cases of refusal of licence. The authors of this suggestion propose that the Lord Chamberlain shall choose one umpire and the author another. The two umpires shall then elect a referee, whose decision shall be final.

This proposal is not likely to be entertained by constitutional lawyers. It is a naïve offer to accept the method of arbitration in what is essentially a matter, not between one private individual or body and another, but between a public offender and the State. It will presumably be ruled out as a proposal to refer a case of manslaughter to arbitration would be ruled out. But even if it were constitutionally sound, it bears all the marks of that practical inexperience which leads men to believe that arbitration either costs nothing or is at least cheaper than law. Who is to pay for the time of the three arbitrators, presumably men of high professional standing? The author may not be able: the manager may not be willing: neither of them should be called upon to pay for a public service otherwise than by their contributions to the revenue. Clearly the State should pay. But even so, the difficulties are only beginning. A licence is seldom refused except on grounds which are controversial. The two arbitrators selected by the opposed parties to the controversy are to agree to leave the decision to a third party unanimously chosen by themselves. That is very far from being a simple solution. An attempt to shorten and simplify the passing of the Finance Bill by referring it to an arbitrator chosen unanimously by Mr Asquith and Mr Balfour might not improbably cost more and last longer than a civil war. And why should the chosen referee – if he ever succeeded in getting chosen – be assumed to be a safer authority than the Examiner of Plays? He would certainly be a less responsible one: in fact, being (however eminent) a casual person called in to settle a single case, he would be virtually irresponsible. Worse still, he would take all responsibility away from the Lord Chamberlain, who is at least an official of the King's Household and a nominee of the Government. The Lord Chamberlain, with all his shortcomings, thinks twice before he refuses a licence, knowing that his refusal is final and may promptly be made public. But if he could transfer his responsibility to an arbitrator, he would naturally do so whenever he felt the slightest misgiving, or whenever, for diplomatic reasons, the licence would come more gracefully from an authority unconnected with the court. These considerations, added to the general objection to the principle of censorship, seem sufficient to put the arbitration expedient quite out of the question.

END OF THE FIRST PART OF THE REJECTED STATEMENT

THE REJECTED STATEMENT – PART II

THE LICENSING OF THEATRES

THE DISTINCTION BETWEEN LICENSING AND CENSORSHIP

It must not be concluded that the uncompromising abolition of all censorship involves the abandonment of all control and regulation of theatres. Factories are regulated in the public interest; but there is no censorship of factories. For example, many persons are sincerely convinced that cotton clothing is unhealthy; that alcoholic drinks are demoralizing; and that playing-cards are the devil's picture-books. But though the factories in which cotton, whiskey, and cards are manufactured are stringently regulated under the factory code and the Public Health and Building Acts, the inspectors appointed to carry out these Acts never go to a manufacturer and inform him that unless he manufactures woollens instead of cottons, ginger-beer instead of whiskey, Bibles instead of playing-cards, he will be forbidden to place his products on the market. In the case of premises licensed for the sale of spirits the authorities go a step further. A public-house differs from a factory in the essential particular that whereas disorder in a factory is promptly and voluntarily suppressed, because every moment of its duration involves a measurable pecuniary loss to the proprietor, disorder in a public-house may be a source of profit to the proprietor by its attraction for disorderly customers. Consequently a publican is compelled to obtain a licence to pursue his trade; and this licence lasts only a year, and need not be renewed if his house has been conducted in a disorderly manner in the meantime.

PROSTITUTION AND DRINK IN THEATRES

The theatre presents the same problem as the public-house in respect to disorder. To begin with, a theatre is actually a place licensed for the sale of spirits. The bars at a London theatre can be let without difficulty for £30 a week and upwards. And though it is clear that nobody will pay from a shilling to half a guinea for access to a theatre bar when he can obtain access to an ordinary public-house for nothing, there is no law to prevent the theatre proprietor from issuing free passes broadcast and recouping himself by the profit on the sale of drink. Besides, there may be some other attraction than the sale of drink. When this attraction is that of the play no objection need be made. But it happens that the auditorium of a theatre, with its brilliant lighting and luxurious decorations, makes a very effective shelter and background for the display of fine dresses and pretty faces. Consequently theatres have been used for centuries in England as markets by prostitutes. From the Restoration to the days of Macready all theatres were made use of in this way as a matter of course; and to this, far more than to any prejudice against dramatic art, we owe the Puritan formula that the theatre door is the gate of hell. Macready had a hard struggle to drive the prostitutes from his theatre; and since his time the London theatres controlled by the Lord Chamberlain have become respectable and even socially pretentious. But some of the variety theatres still derive a revenue by selling admissions to women who do not look at the performance, and men who go to purchase or admire the women. And in the provinces this state of things is by no means confined to the variety theatres. The real attraction is sometimes not the performance at all. The theatre is not really a theatre: it is a drink shop and a prostitution market; and the last shred of its disguise is stripped by the virtually indiscriminate issue of free tickets to the men. Access to the stage is also easily obtained; and the plays preferred by the management are those in which the stage is filled with young women who are not in any serious technical sense of the word actresses at all. Considering that all this is now possible at any theatre, and actually occurs at some theatres, the fact that our best theatres are as respectable as they are is much to their credit; but it is still an intolerable evil that respectable managers should have to fight against the free tickets and disorderly housekeeping of unscrupulous competitors. The dramatic author is equally injured. He finds that unless he writes plays which make suitable sideshows for drinking-bars and brothels, he may be excluded from towns where there is not room for two theatres, and where the one existing theatre is exploiting drunkenness and prostitution instead of carrying on a legitimate dramatic business. Indeed everybody connected with the theatrical profession suffers in reputation from the detestable tradition of such places, against which the censorship has proved quite useless.

Here we have a strong case for applying either the licensing system or whatever better means may be devized for securing the orderly conduct of houses of public entertainment, dramatic or other. Liberty must, no doubt, be respected in so far that no manager should have the right to refuse admission to decently dressed, sober, and well-conducted persons, whether they are prostitutes, soldiers in uniform, gentlemen not in evening dress, Indians, or what not; but when disorder is stopped, disorderly persons will either cease to come or else reform their manners. It is, however, quite arguable that the indiscriminate issue of free admissions, though an apparently innocent and good-natured, and certainly a highly popular proceeding, should expose the proprietor of the theatre to the risk of a refusal to renew his licence.

WHY THE MANAGERS DREAD LOCAL CONTROL

All this points to the transfer of the control of theatres from the Lord Chamberlain to the municipality. And this step is opposed by the long-run managers, partly because they take it for granted that municipal control must involve municipal censorship of plays, so that plays might be licensed in one town and prohibited in the next, and partly because, as they have no desire to produce plays which are in advance of public opinion, and as the Lord Chamberlain in every other respect gives more scandal by his laxity than trouble by his severity, they find in the present system a cheap and easy means of procuring a certificate which relieves them of all social responsibility, and provides them with so strong a weapon of defence in case of a prosecution that it acts in practice as a bar to any such proceedings. Above all, they know that the Examiner of Plays is free from the pressure of that large body of English public opinion already alluded to, which regards the theatre as the Prohibitionist Teetotaller regards the public-house: that is, as an abomination to be stamped out unconditionally. The managers rightly dread this pressure more than anything else; and they believe that it is so strong in local governments as to be a characteristic bias of municipal authority. In this they are no doubt mistaken. There is not a municipal authority of any importance in the country in which a proposal to stamp out the theatre, or even to treat it illiberally, would have a chance of adoption. Municipal control of the variety theatres (formerly called music halls) has been very far from illiberal, except in the one particular in which the Lord Chamberlain is equally illiberal. That particular is the assumption that a draped figure is decent and an undraped one indecent. It is useless to point to actual experience, which proves abundantly that naked or apparently naked figures, whether exhibited as living pictures, animated statuary, or in a dance, are at their best not only innocent, but refining in their effect, whereas those actresses and skirt dancers who have brought the peculiar aphrodisiac effect which is objected to to the highest pitch of efficiency wear twice as many petticoats as an ordinary lady does, and seldom exhibit more than their ankles. Unfortunately, municipal councillors persist in confusing decency with drapery; and both in London and the provinces certain positively edifying performances have been forbidden or withdrawn under pressure, and replaced by coarse and vicious ones. There is not the slightest reason to suppose that the Lord Chamberlain would have been any more tolerant; but this does not alter the fact that the municipal licensing authorities have actually used their powers to set up a censorship which is open to all the objections to censorship in general, and which, in addition, sets up the objection from which central control is free: namely, the impossibility of planning theatrical tours without the serious commercial risk of having the performance forbidden in some of the towns booked. How can this be prevented?

DESIRABLE LIMITATIONS OF LOCAL CONTROL

The problem is not a difficult one. The municipality can be limited just as the monarchy is limited. The Act transferring theatres to local control can be a charter of the liberties of the stage as well as an Act to reform administration. The power to refuse to grant or renew a licence to a theatre need not be an arbitrary one. The municipality may be required to state the ground of refusal; and certain grounds can be expressly declared as unlawful; so that it shall be possible for the manager to resort to the courts for a mandamus to compel the authority to grant a licence. It can be declared unlawful for a licensing authority to demand from the manager any disclosure of the nature of any entertainment he proposes to give, or to prevent its performance, or to refuse to renew his licence on the ground that the tendency of his entertainments is contrary to religion and morals, or that the theatre is an undesirable institution, or that there are already as many theatres as are needed, or that the theatre draws people away from the churches, chapels, mission halls, and the like in its neighborhood. The assumption should be that every citizen has a right to open and conduct a theatre, and therefore has a right to a licence unless he has forfeited that right by allowing his theatre to become a disorderly house, or failing to provide a building which complies with the regulations concerning sanitation and egress in case of fire, or being convicted of an offence against public decency. Also, the licensing powers of the authority should not be delegated to any official or committee; and the manager or lessee of the theatre should have a right to appear in person or by counsel to plead against any motion to refuse to grant or renew his licence. With these safeguards the licensing power could not be stretched to censorship. The manager would enjoy liberty of conscience as far as the local authority is concerned; but on the least attempt on his part to keep a disorderly house under cover of opening a theatre he would risk his licence.

But the managers will not and should not be satisfied with these limits to the municipal power. If they are deprived of the protection of the Lord Chamberlain's licence, and at the same time efficiently protected against every attempt at censorship by the licensing authority, the enemies of the theatre will resort to the ordinary law, and try to get from the prejudices of a jury what they are debarred from getting from the prejudices of a County Council or City Corporation. Moral Reform Societies, 'Purity' Societies, Vigilance Societies, exist in England and America for the purpose of enforcing the existing laws against obscenity, blasphemy, Sabbath-breaking, the debauchery of children, prostitution, and so forth. The paid officials of these societies, in their anxiety to produce plenty of evidence of their activity in the annual reports which go out to the subscribers, do not always discriminate between an obscene postcard and an artistic one, or to put it more exactly, between a naked figure and an indecent one. They often combine a narrow but terribly sincere sectarian bigotry with a complete ignorance of art and history. Even when they have some culture, their livelihood is at the mercy of subscribers and committee men who have none. If these officials had any power of distinguishing between art and blackguardism, between morality and virtue, between immorality and vice, between conscientious heresy and mere baseness of mind and foulness of mouth, they might be trusted by theatrical managers not to abuse the powers of the common informer. As it is, it has been found necessary, in order to enable good music to be performed on Sunday, to take away these powers in that particular, and vest them solely in the Attorney-General. This disqualification of the common informer should be extended to the initiation of all proceedings of a censorial character against theatres. Few people are aware of the monstrous laws against blasphemy which still disgrace our statute book. If any serious attempt were made to carry them out, prison accommodation would have to be provided for almost every educated person in the country, beginning with the Archbishop of Canterbury. Until some government with courage and character enough to repeal them comes into power, it is not too much to ask that such infamous powers of oppression should be kept in responsible hands and not left at the disposal of every bigot ignorant enough to be unaware of the social dangers of persecution. Besides, the common informer is not always a sincere bigot who believes he is performing an action of signal merit in silencing and ruining a heretic. He is unfortunately just as often a blackmailer, who has studied his powers as a common informer in order that he may extort money for refraining from exercising them. If the manager is to be responsible he should be made responsible to a responsible functionary. To be responsible to every fanatical ignoramus who chooses to prosecute him for exhibiting a cast of the Hermes of Praxiteles in his vestibule, or giving a performance of Measure for Measure, is mere slavery. It is made bearable at present by the protection of the Lord Chamberlain's certificate. But when that is no longer available, the common informer must be disarmed if the manager is to enjoy security.

SUMMARY OF THE REJECTED STATEMENT

The general case against censorship as a principle, and the particular case against the existing English censorship and against its replacement by a more enlightened one, is now complete. The following is a recapitulation of the propositions and conclusions contended for.

1. The question of censorship or no censorship is a question of high political principle and not of petty policy.

2. The toleration of heresy and shocks to morality on the stage, and even their protection against the prejudices and superstitions which necessarily enter largely into morality and public opinion, are essential to the welfare of the nation.

3. The existing censorship of the Lord Chamberlain does not only intentionally suppress heresy and challenges to morality in their serious and avowed forms, but unintentionally gives the special protection of its official licence to the most extreme impropriety that the lowest section of London playgoers will tolerate in theatres especially devoted to their entertainment, licensing

everything that is popular and forbidding any attempt to change public opinion or morals.

4. The Lord Chamberlain's censorship is open to the special objection that its application to political plays is taken to indicate the attitude of the Crown on questions of domestic and foreign policy, and that it imposes the limits of etiquet on the historical drama.

5. A censorship of a more enlightened and independent kind, exercised by the most eminent available authorities, would prove in practice more disastrous than the censorship of the Lord Chamberlain, because the more eminent its members were the less possible would it be for them to accept the responsibility for heresy or immorality by licensing them, and because the many heretical and immoral plays which now pass the Lord Chamberlain because he does not understand them, would be understood and suppressed by a more highly enlightened censorship.

6. A reconstructed and enlightened censorship would be armed with summary and effective powers which would stop the evasions by which heretical and immoral plays are now performed in spite of the Lord Chamberlain; and such powers would constitute a tyranny which would ruin the theatre spiritually by driving all independent thinkers from the drama into the uncensored forms of art.

7. The work of critically examining all stage plays in their written form, and of witnessing their performance in order to see that the sense is not altered by the stage business, would, even if it were divided among so many officials as to be physically possible, be mentally impossible to persons of taste and enlightenment.

8. Regulation of theatres is an entirely different matter from censorship, inasmuch as a theatre, being not only a stage, but a place licensed for the sale of spirits, and a public resort capable of being put to disorderly use, and needing special provision for the safety of audiences in cases of fire, etc., cannot be abandoned wholly to private control, and may therefore reasonably be made subject to an annual licence like those now required before allowing premises to be used publicly for music and dancing.

9. In order to prevent the powers of the licensing authority being abused so as to constitute a virtual censorship, any Act

transferring the theatres to the control of a licensing authority should be made also a charter of the rights of dramatic authors and managers by the following provisions:

A. The public prosecutor (the Attorney-General) alone should have the right to set the law in operation against the manager of a theatre or the author of a play in respect of the character of the play or entertainment.

B. No disclosure of the particulars of a theatrical entertainment shall be required before performance.

C. Licences shall not be withheld on the ground that the existence of theatres is dangerous to religion and morals, or on the ground that any entertainment given or contemplated is heretical or immoral.

D. The licensing area shall be no less than that of a County Council or City Corporation, which shall not delegate its licensing powers to any minor local authority or to any official or committee; it shall decide all questions affecting the existence of a theatrical licence by vote of the entire body; managers, lessees, and proprietors of theatres shall have the right to plead, in person or by counsel, against a proposal to withhold a licence; and the licence shall not be withheld except for stated reasons, the validity of which shall be subject to the judgment of the high courts.

E. The annual licence, once granted, shall not be cancelled or suspended unless the manager has been convicted by public prosecution of an offence against the ordinary laws against disorderly housekeeping, indecency, blasphemy, etc., except in cases where some structural or sanitary defect in the building necessitates immediate action for the protection of the public against physical injury.

F. No licence shall be refused on the ground that the proximity of the theatre to a church, mission hall, school, or other place of worship, edification, instruction, or entertainment (including another theatre) would draw the public away from such places into its own doors.

PREFACE RESUMED

MR GEORGE ALEXANDER'S PROTEST

On the facts mentioned in the foregoing statement, and in my evidence before the Joint Select Committee, no controversy arose except on one point. Mr George Alexander protested vigorously and indignantly against my admission that theatres, like public-houses, need special control on the ground that they can profit by disorder, and are sometimes conducted with that end in view. Now, Mr Alexander is a famous actor-manager; and it is very difficult to persuade the public that the more famous an actor-manager is the less he is likely to know about any theatre except his own. When the Committee of 1892 reported, I was considered guilty of a perverse paradox when I said that the witness who knew least about the theatre was Henry Irving. Yet a moment's consideration would have shewn that the paradox was a platitude. For about quarter of a century Irving was confined night after night to his own theatre and his own dressing-room, never seeing a play even there because he was himself part of the play; producing the works of long departed authors; and, to the extent to which his talent was extraordinary, necessarily making his theatre unlike any other theatre. When he went to the provinces or to America, the theatres to which he went were swept and garnished for him, and their staffs replaced – as far as he came in contact with them – by his own lieutenants. In the end, there was hardly a first-nighter in his gallery who did not know more about the London theatres and the progress of dramatic art than he; and as to the provinces, if any chief constable had told him the real history and character of many provincial theatres, he would have denounced that chief constable as an ignorant libeller of a noble profession. But the constable would have been right for all that. Now if this was true of Sir Henry Irving, who did not become a London manager until he had roughed it for years in the provinces, how much more true must it be of, say, Mr George Alexander, whose successful march through his profession has passed as far from the purlieus of our theatrical world as the king's naval career from the Isle of Dogs? The moment we come to that necessary part of the censorship question which deals with the control of theatres from the point of view of those who know how much money can be made out of them by managers who seek to make the auditorium attractive rather than the stage, you find the managers divided into two sections. The first section consists of honorable and successful managers like Mr Alexander, who know nothing of such abuses, and deny, with perfect sincerity and indignant vehemence, that they exist except, perhaps, in certain notorious variety theatres. The other is the silent section which knows better, but is very well content to be publicly defended and privately amused by Mr Alexander's innocence. To accept a West End manager as an expert in theatres because he is an actor is much as if we were to accept the organist of St Paul's Cathedral as an expert on music halls because he is a musician. The real experts are all in the conspiracy to keep the police out of the theatre. And they are so successful that even the police do not know as much as they should.

The police should have been examined by the Committee, and the whole question of the extent to which theatres are disorderly houses in disguise sifted to the bottom. For it is on this point that we discover behind the phantoms of the corrupt dramatists who are restrained by the censorship from debauching the stage, the reality of the corrupt managers and theatre proprietors who actually do debauch it without let or hindrance from the censorship. The whole case for giving control over theatres to local authorities rests on this reality.

ELIZA AND HER BATH

The persistent notion that a theatre is an Alsatia where the king's writ does not run, and where any wickedness is possible in the absence of a special tribunal and a special police, was brought out by an innocent remark made by Sir William Gilbert, who, when giving evidence before the Committee, was asked by Colonel Lockwood whether a law sufficient to restrain impropriety in books would also restrain impropriety in plays. Sir William replied: 'I should say there is a very wide distinction between what is read and what is seen. In a novel one may read that "Eliza stripped off her dressing-gown and stepped into her bath'' without any harm; but I think if that were presented on the stage it would be shocking.' All the stupid and inconsiderate people seized eagerly on this illustration as if it were a successful attempt to prove that without a censorship we should be unable to prevent actresses from appearing naked on the stage. As a matter of fact, if an actress could be persuaded to do such a thing (and it would be about as easy to persuade a bishop's wife to appear in church in the same condition) the police would simply arrest her on a charge of indecent exposure. The extent to which this obvious safeguard was overlooked may be taken as a measure of the thoughtlessness and frivolity of the excuses made for the censorship. It should be added that the artistic representation of a bath, with every suggestion of nakedness that the law as to decency allows, is one of the most familiar subjects of scenic art. From the Rhine maidens in Wagner's Trilogy, and the bathers in the second act of Les Huguenots, to the ballets of water nymphs in our Christmas pantomimes and at our variety theatres, the sound hygienic propaganda of the bath, and the charm of the undraped human figure, are exploited without offence on the stage to an extent never dreamt of by any novelist.

A KING'S PROCTOR

Another hare was started by Professor Gilbert Murray and Mr Laurence Housman, who, in pure kindness to the managers, asked whether it would not be possible to establish for their assistance a sort of King's Proctor to whom plays might be referred for an official legal opinion as to their compliance with the law before production. There are several objections to this proposal; and they may as well be stated in case the proposal should be revived. In the first place, no lawyer with the most elementary knowledge of the law of libel in its various applications to sedition, obscenity, and blasphemy, could answer for the consequences of producing any play whatsoever as to which the smallest question could arise in the mind of any sane person. I have been a critic and an author in active service for thirty years; and though nothing I have written has ever been prosecuted in England or made the subject of legal proceedings, yet I have never published in my life an article, a play, or a book, as to which, if I had taken legal advice, an expert could have assured me that I was proof against prosecution or against an action for damages by the persons criticized. No doubt a sensible solicitor might have advised me that the risk was no greater than all men have to take in dangerous trades; but such an opinion, though it may encourage a client, does not protect him. For example, if a publisher asks his solicitor whether he may venture on an edition of Sterne's Sentimental Journey, or a manager whether he may produce King Lear without risk of prosecution, the solicitor will advise him to go ahead. But if the solicitor or counsel consulted by him were asked for a guarantee that neither of these works was a libel, he would have to reply that he could give no such guarantee; that, on the contrary, it was his duty to warn his client that both of them are obscene libels; that King Lear, containing as it does perhaps the most appalling blasphemy that despair ever uttered, is a blasphemous libel, and that it is doubtful whether it could not be construed as a seditious libel as well. As to Ibsen's Brand (the play which made him popular with the most earnestly religious people) no sane solicitor would advise his client even to chance it except in a broadly cultivated and tolerant (or indifferent) modern city. The lighter plays would be no better off. What lawyer could accept any responsibility for the production of Sardou's Divorçons or Clyde Fitch's The Woman in the Case? Put the proposed King's Proctor in operation tomorrow; and what will be the result? The managers will find that instead of insuring them as the Lord Chamberlain does, he will warn them that every play they submit to him is vulnerable to the law, and that they must produce it not only on the ordinary risk of acting on their own responsibility, but at the very grave additional risk of doing so in the teeth of an official warning. Under such circumstances, what manager would resort a second time to the Proctor; and how would the Proctor live without fees, unless indeed the Government gave him a salary for doing nothing? The institution would not last a year, except as a job for somebody.

COUNSEL'S OPINION

The proposal is still less plausible when it is considered that at present, without any new legislation at all, any manager who is doubtful about a play can obtain the advice of his solicitor, or Counsel's opinion, if he thinks it will be of any service to him. The verdict of the proposed King's Proctor would be nothing but Counsel's opinion without the liberty of choice of Counsel, possibly cheapened, but sure to be adverse; for an official cannot give practical advice as a friend and a man of the world; he must stick to the letter of the law and take no chances. And as far as the law is concerned, journalism, literature, and the drama exist only by custom or sufferance.

WANTED: A NEW MAGNA CHARTA

This leads us to a very vital question. Is it not possible to amend the law so as to make it possible for a lawyer to advise his client that he may publish the works of Blake, Zola, and Swinburne, or produce the plays of Ibsen and Mr Granville Barker, or print an ordinary criticism in his newspaper, without the possibility of finding himself in prison, or mulcted in damages and costs in consequence? No doubt it is; but only by a declaration of constitutional right to blaspheme, rebel, and deal with tabooed subjects. Such a declaration is not just now within the scope of practical politics, although we are compelled to act to a great extent as if it was actually part of the constitution. All that can be done is to take my advice and limit the necessary public control of the theatres in such a manner as to prevent its being abused as a censorship. We have ready to hand the machinery of licensing as applied to public-houses. A licensed victualler can now be assured confidently by his lawyer that a magistrate cannot refuse to renew his licence on the ground that he (the magistrate) is a teetotaller and has seen too much of the evil of drink to sanction its sale. The magistrate must give a judicial reason for his refusal, meaning really a constitutional reason; and his teetotalism is not such a reason. In the same way you can protect a theatrical manager by ruling out certain reasons as unconstitutional, as suggested in my statement. Combine this with the abolition of the common informer's power to initiate proceedings; and you will have gone as far as seems possible at present. You will have local control of the theatres for police purposes and sanitary purposes without censorship; and I do not see what more is possible until we get a formal Magna Charta declaring all the categories of libel and the blasphemy laws contrary to public liberty, and repealing and defining accordingly.

PROPOSED: A NEW STAR CHAMBER

Yet we cannot mention Magna Charta without recalling how useless such documents are to a nation which has no more political comprehension nor political virtue than King John. When Henry VII calmly proceeded to tear up Magna Charta by establishing the Star Chamber (a criminal court consisting of a committee of the Privy Council without a jury) nobody objected until, about a century and a half later, the Star Chamber began cutting off the ears of eminent Nonconformist divines and standing them in the pillory; and then the Nonconformists, and nobody else, abolished the Star Chamber. And if anyone doubts that we are quite ready to establish the Star Chamber again, let him read the Report of the Joint Select Committee, on which I now venture to offer a few criticisms.

The report of the Committee, which will be found in the Blue book, should be read with attention and respect as far as page x, up to which point it is an able and well-written statement of the case. From page x onward, when it goes on from diagnosing the disease to prescribing the treatment, it should be read with even greater attention but with no respect whatever, as the main object of the treatment is to conciliate the How Not To Do It majority. It contains, however, one very notable proposal, the same being nothing more or less than to revive the Star Chamber for the purpose of dealing with heretical or seditious plays and their authors, and indeed with all charges against theatrical entertainments except common police cases of indecency. The reason given is that for which the Star Chamber was created by Henry VII: that is, the inadequacy of the ordinary law. 'We consider,' says the report, 'that the law which prevents or punishes indecency, blasphemy and libel in printed publications [it does not, by the way, except in the crudest police cases] would not be adequate for the control of the drama.' Therefore a committee of the Privy Council is to be empowered to suppress plays and punish managers and authors at its pleasure, on the motion of the Attorney-General, without a jury. The members of the Committee will, of course, be men of high standing and character: otherwise they would not be on the Privy Council. That is to say, they will have all the qualifications of Archbishop Laud.

Now I have no guarantee that any member of the majority of the Joint Select Committee ever heard of the Star Chamber or of Archbishop Laud. One of them did not know that politics meant anything more than party electioneering. Nothing is more alarming than the ignorance of our public men of the commonplaces of our history, and their consequent readiness to repeat experiments which have in the past produced national catastrophes. At all events, whether they knew what they were doing or not, there can be no question as to what they did. They proposed virtually that the Act of the Long Parliament in 1641 shall be repealed, and the Star Chamber re-established, in order that playwrights and managers may be punished for unspecified offences unknown to the law. When I say unspecified, I should say specified as follows (see page xi of the report) in the case of a play:

(*a*) To be indecent.

(*b*) To contain offensive personalities.

(*c*) To represent on the stage in an invidious manner a living person, or any person recently dead.

(*d*) To do violence to the sentiment of religious reverence.

(*e*) To be calculated to conduce to vice or crime.

(*f*) To be calculated to impair friendly relations with any foreign power.

(*g*) To be calculated to cause a breach of the peace.

Now it is clear that there is no play yet written, or possible to be written, in this world, that might not be condemned under one or other of these heads. How any sane man, not being a professed enemy of public liberty, could put his hand to so monstrous a catalogue passes my understanding. Had a comparatively definite and innocent clause been added forbidding the affirmation or denial of the doctrine of Transubstantiation, the country would have been up in arms at once. Lord Ribblesdale made an effort to reduce the seven categories to the old formula 'not to be fitting for the preservation of good manners, decorum, or the public peace'; but this proposal was not carried; whilst on Lord Gorell's motion a final widening of the net was achieved by adding the phrase 'to be calculated to'; so that even if a play does not produce any of the results feared, the author can still be punished on the ground that his play is 'calculated' to produce them. I have no hesitation in saying that a committee capable of such an outrageous display of thoughtlessness and historical ignorance as this paragraph of its report implies deserves to be haled before the tribunal it has itself proposed, and dealt with under a general clause levelled at conduct 'calculated to' overthrow the liberties of England.

POSSIBILITIES OF THE PROPOSAL

Still, though I am certainly not willing to give Lord Gorell the chance of seeing me in the pillory with my ears cut off if I can help it, I daresay many authors would rather take their chance with a Star Chamber than with a jury, just as some soldiers would rather take their chance with a court-martial than at Quarter Sessions. For that matter, some of them would rather take their chance with the Lord Chamberlain than with either. And though this is no reason for depriving the whole body of authors of the benefit of Magna Charta, still, if the right of the proprietor of a play to refuse the good offices of the Privy Council and to perform the play until his accusers had indicted him at law, and obtained the verdict of a jury against him, were sufficiently guarded, the proposed Committee might be set up and used for certain purposes. For instance, it might be made a condition of the intervention of the Attorney-General or the Director of Public Prosecutions that he should refer an accused play to the Committee, and obtain their sanction before taking action, offering the proprietor of the play, if the Committee thought fit, an opportunity of voluntarily accepting trial by the Committee as an alternative to prosecution in the ordinary course of law. But the Committee should have no powers of punishment beyond the power (formidable enough) of suspending performances of the play. If it thought that additional punishment was called for, it could order a prosecution without allowing the proprietor or author of the play the alternative of a trial by itself. The author of the play should be made a party to all proceedings of the Committee, and have the right to defend himself in person or by counsel. This would provide a check on the Attorney-General (who might be as bigoted as any of the municipal aldermen who are so much dreaded by the actor-managers) without enabling the Committee to abuse its powers for party, class, or sectarian ends beyond that irreducible minimum of abuse which a popular jury would endorse, for which minimum there is no remedy.

But when everything is said for the Star Chamber that can be said, and every precaution taken to secure to those whom it pursues the alternative of trial by jury, the expedient still remains a very questionable one, to be endured for the sake of its protective rather than its repressive powers. It should abolish the present quaint toleration of rioting in theatres. For example, if it is to be an offence to perform a play which the proposed new Committee shall condemn, it should also be made an offence to disturb a performance which the Committee has not condemned. 'Brawling' at a theatre should be dealt with as severely as brawling in church if the censorship is to be taken out of the hands of the public. At present Jenny Geddes may throw her stool at the head of a playwright who preaches unpalatable doctrine to her, or rather, since her stool is a fixture, she may hiss and hoot and make it impossible to proceed with the performance, even although nobody has compelled her to come to the theatre or suspended her liberty to stay away, and although she has no claim on an unendowed theatre for her spiritual necessities, as she has on her parish church. If mob censorship cannot be trusted to keep naughty playwrights in order, still less can it be trusted to keep the pioneers of thought in countenance; and I submit that anyone hissing a play permitted by the new censorship should be guilty of contempt of court.

STAR CHAMBER SENTIMENTALITY

But what is most to be dreaded in a Star Chamber is not its sternness but its sentimentality. There is no worse censorship than one which considers only the feelings of the spectators, except perhaps one which considers the feelings of people who do not even witness the performance. Take the case of the Passion Play at Oberammergau. The offence given by a representation of the Crucifixion on the stage is not bounded by frontiers: further, it is an offence of which the voluntary spectators are guilty no less than the actors. If it is to be tolerated at all: if we are not to make war on the German Empire for permitting it, nor punish the English people who go to Bavaria to see it and thereby endow it with English money, we may as well tolerate it in London, where nobody need go to see it except those who are not offended by it. When Wagner's Parsifal becomes available for representation in London, many people will be sincerely horrified when the miracle of the Mass is simulated on the stage of Covent Garden, and the Holy Ghost descends in the form of a dove. But if the Committee of the Privy Council, or the Lord Chamberlain, or anyone else, were to attempt to keep Parsifal from us to spare the feelings of these people, it would not be long before even the most thoughtless champions of the censorship would see that the principle of doing nothing that could shock anybody had reduced itself to absurdity. No quarter whatever should be given to the bigotry of people so unfit for social life as to insist not only that their own prejudices and superstitions should have the fullest toleration but that everybody else should be compelled to think and act as they do. Every service in St Paul's Cathedral is an outrage to the opinions of the congregation of the Roman Catholic Cathedral of Westminster. Every Liberal meeting is a defiance and a challenge to the most cherished opinions of the Unionists. A law to compel the Roman Catholics to attend service at St Paul's, or the Liberals to attend the meetings of the Primrose League would be resented as an insufferable tyranny. But a law to shut up both St Paul's and the Westminster Cathedral, and to put down political meetings and associations because of the offence given by them to many worthy and excellent people, would be a far worse tyranny, because it would kill the religious and political life of the country outright, whereas to compel people to attend the services and meetings of their opponents would greatly enlarge their minds, and would actually be a good thing if it were enforced all round. I should not object to a law to compel everybody to read two newspapers, each violently opposed to the other in politics; but to forbid us to read newspapers at all would be to maim us mentally and cashier our country in the ranks of civilization. I deny that anybody has the right to demand more from me, over and above lawful conduct in a general sense, than liberty to stay away from the theatre in which my plays are represented. If he is unfortunate enough to have a religion so petty that it can be insulted (any man is as welcome to insult my religion, if he can, as he is to insult the universe) I claim the right to insult it to my heart's content, if I choose, provided I do not compel him to come and hear me. If I think this country ought to make war on any other country, then, so long as war remains lawful, I claim full liberty to write and perform a play inciting the country to that war without interference from the ambassadors of the menaced country. I may 'give pain to many worthy people, and pleasure to none', as the Censor's pet phrase puts it: I may even make Europe a cockpit and Asia a shambles: no matter: if preachers and politicians, statesmen and soldiers, may do these things – if it is right that such things should be done, then I claim my share in the right to do them. If the proposed Committee is meant to prevent me from doing these things whilst men of other professions are permitted to do them, then I protest with all my might against the formation of such a Committee. If it is to protect me, on the contrary, against the attacks that bigots and corrupt pornographers may make on me by appealing to the ignorance and prejudices of common jurors, then I welcome it; but is that really the object of its proposers? And if it is, what guarantee have I that the new tribunal will not presently resolve into a mere committee to avoid unpleasantness and keep the stage 'in good taste'? It is no more possible for me to do my work honestly as a playwright without giving pain than it is for a dentist. The nation's morals are like its teeth: the more decayed they are the more it hurts to touch them. Prevent dentists and dramatists from giving pain, and not only will our morals become as carious as our teeth, but toothache and the plagues that follow neglected morality will presently cause more agony than all the dentists and dramatists at their worst have caused since the world began.

ANYTHING FOR A QUIET LIFE

Another doubt: would a Committee of the Privy Council really face the risks that must be taken by all communities as the price of our freedom to evolve? Would it not rather take the popular English view that freedom and virtue generally are sweet and desirable only when they cost nothing? Nothing worth having is to be had without risk. A mother risks her child's life every time she lets it ramble through the countryside, or cross the street or clamber over the rocks on the shore by itself. A father risks his son's morals when he gives him a latchkey. The members of the Joint Select Committee risked my producing a revolver and shooting them when they admitted me to the room without having me handcuffed. And these risks are no unreal ones. Every day some child is maimed or drowned and some young man infected with disease; and political assassinations have been appallingly frequent of late years. Railway travelling has its risks; motoring has its risks; aeroplaning has its risks; every advance we make costs us a risk of some sort. And though these are only risks to the individual, to the community they are certainties. It is not certain that I will be killed this year in a railway accident; but it is certain that somebody will. The invention of printing and the freedom of the press have brought upon us, not merely risks of their abuse, but the establishment as part of our social routine of some of the worst evils a community can suffer from. People who realize these evils shriek for the suppression of motor cars, the virtual imprisonment and enslavement of the young, the passing of Press Laws (especially in Egypt, India, and Ireland), exactly as they shriek for a censorship of the stage. The freedom of the stage will be abused just as certainly as the complaisance and innocence of the censorship is abused at present. It will also be used by writers like myself for raising very difficult and disturbing questions, social, political, and religious, at moments which may be extremely inconvenient to the government. Is it certain that a Committee of the Privy Council would stand up to all this as the price of liberty? I doubt it. If I am to be at the mercy of a nice amiable Committee of elderly gentlemen (I know all about elderly gentlemen, being one myself) whose motto is the highly popular one, 'Anything for a quiet life,' and who will make the inevitable abuses of freedom by our blackguards an excuse for interfering with any disquieting use of it by myself, then I shall be worse off than I am with the Lord Chamberlain, whose mind is not broad enough to obstruct the whole range of thought. If it were, he would be given a more difficult post.

SHALL THE EXAMINER OF PLAYS STARVE?

And here I may be reminded that if I prefer the Lord Chamberlain I can go to the Lord Chamberlain, who is to retain all his present functions for the benefit of those who prefer to be judged by him. But I am not so sure that the Lord Chamberlain will be able to exercise those functions for long if resort to him is to be optional. Let me be kinder to him than he has been to me, and uncover for him the pitfalls which the Joint Select Committee have dug (and concealed) in his path. Consider how the voluntary system must inevitably work. The Joint Select Committee expressly urges that the Lord Chamberlain's licence must not be a bar to a prosecution. Granted that in spite of this reservation the licence would prove in future as powerful a defence as it has been in the past, yet the voluntary clause nevertheless places the manager at the mercy of any author who makes it a condition of his contract that his play shall not be submitted for licence. I should probably take that course without opposition from the manager. For the manager, knowing that three of my plays have been refused a licence, and that it would be far safer to produce a play for which no licence had been asked than one for which it had been asked and refused, would agree that it was more prudent, in my case, to avail himself of the power of dispensing with the Lord Chamberlain's licence. But now mark the consequences. The manager, having thus discovered that his best policy was to dispense with the licence in the few doubtful cases, would presently ask himself why he should spend two guineas each on licences for the many plays as to which no question could conceivably arise. What risk does any manager run in producing such works as Sweet Lavender, Peter Pan, The Silver King, or any of the 99 per cent of plays that are equally neutral on controversial questions. Does anyone seriously believe that the managers would continue to pay the Lord Chamberlain two guineas a play out of mere love and loyalty, only to create an additional risk in the case of controversial plays, and to guard against risks that do not exist in the case of the great bulk of other productions? Only those would remain faithful to him who produce such plays as the Select Committee began by discussing *in camera*, and ended by refusing to discuss at all because they were too nasty. These people would still try to get a licence, and would still no doubt succeed as they do today. But could the King's Reader of Plays live on his fees from these plays alone; and if he could how long would his post survive the discredit of licensing only pornographic plays? It is clear to me that the Examiner would be starved out of existence, and the censorship perish of desuetude. Perhaps that is exactly what the Select Committee contemplated. If so, I have nothing more to say, except that I think sudden death would be more merciful.

LORD GORELL'S AWAKENING

In the meantime, conceive the situation which would arise if a licensed play were prosecuted. To make it clearer, let us imagine any other offender – say a company promoter with a fraudulent prospectus – pleading in Court that he had induced the Lord Chamberlain to issue a certificate that the prospectus contained nothing objectionable, and that on the strength of that certificate he issued it; also, that by law the Court could do nothing to him except order him to wind up his company. Some such vision as this must have come to Lord Gorell when he at last grappled seriously with the problem. Mr Harcourt seized the opportunity to make a last rally. He seconded Lord Gorell's proposal that the Committee should admit that its scheme of an optional censorship was an elaborate absurdity, and report that all censorship before production was out of the question. But it was too late: the *volte face* was too sudden and complete. It was Lord Gorell whose vote had turned the close division which took place on the question of receiving my statement. It was Lord Gorell without whose countenance and authority the farce of the books could never have been performed. Yet here was Lord Gorell, after assenting to all the provisions for the optional censorship paragraph by paragraph, suddenly informing his colleagues that they had been wrong all through and that I had been right all through, and inviting them to scrap their work and adopt my conclusion. No wonder Lord Gorell got only one vote: that of Mr Harcourt. But the incident is not the less significant. Lord Gorell carried more weight than any other member of the Committee on the legal and constitutional aspect of the question. Had he begun where he left off – had he at the outset put down his foot on the notion that an optional penal law could ever be anything but a gross contradiction in terms, that part of the Committee's proposals would never have come into existence.

JUDGES: THEIR PROFESSIONAL LIMITATIONS

I do not, however, appeal to Lord Gorell's judgment on all points. It is inevitable that a judge should be deeply impressed by his professional experience with a sense of the impotence of judges and laws and courts to deal satisfactorily with evils which are so Protean and elusive as to defy definition, and which yet seem to present quite simple problems to the common sense of men of the world. You have only to imagine the Privy Council as consisting of men of the world highly endowed with common sense, to persuade yourself that the supplementing of the law by the common sense of the Privy Council would settle the whole difficulty. But no man knows what he means by common sense, though every man can tell you that it is very uncommon, even in Privy Councils. And since every ploughman is a man of the world, it is evident that even the phrase itself does not mean what it says. As a matter of fact, it means in ordinary use simply a man who will not make himself disagreeable for the sake of a principle: just the sort of man who should never be allowed to meddle with political rights. Now to a judge a political right, that is, a dogma which is above our laws and conditions our laws, instead of being subject to them, is anarchic and abhorrent. That is why I trust Lord Gorell when he is defending the integrity of the law against the proposal to make it in any sense optional, whilst I very strongly mistrust him, as I mistrust all professional judges, when political rights are in danger.

CONCLUSION

I must conclude by recommending the Government to take my advice wherever it conflicts with that of the Joint Select Committee. It is, I think, obviously more deeply considered and better informed, though I say it that should not. At all events, I have given my reasons; and at that I must leave it. As the tradition which makes Malvolio not only Master of the Revels but Master of the Mind of England, and which has come down to us from Henry VIII, is manifestly doomed to the dustbin, the sooner it goes there the better; for the democratic control which naturally succeeds it can easily be limited so as to prevent it becoming either a censorship or a tyranny. The Examiner of Plays should receive a generous pension, and be set free to practise privately as an expert adviser of theatrical managers. There is no reason why they should be deprived of the counsel they so highly value.

It only remains to say that public performances of The Shewing-up of Blanco Posnet are still prohibited in Great Britain by the Lord Chamberlain. An attempt was made to prevent even its performance in Ireland by some indiscreet Castle officials in the absence of the Lord Lieutenant. This attempt gave extraordinary publicity to the production of the play; and every possible effort was made to persuade the Irish public that the performance would be an outrage to their religion, and to provoke a repetition of the rioting that attended the first performances of Synge's Playboy of the Western World before the most sensitive and, on provocation, the most turbulent audience in the kingdom. The directors of the

Irish National Theatre, Lady Gregory and Mr William Butler Yeats, rose to the occasion with inspiring courage. I am a conciliatory person, and was willing, as I always am, to make every concession in return for having my own way. But Lady Gregory and Mr Yeats not only would not yield an inch, but insisted, within the due limits of gallant warfare, on taking the field with every circumstance of defiance, and winning the battle with every trophy of victory. Their triumph was as complete as they could have desired. The performance exhausted the possibilities of success, and provoked no murmur, though it inspired several approving sermons. Later on, Lady Gregory and Mr Yeats brought the play to London and performed it under the Lord Chamberlain's nose, through the instrumentality of the Stage Society.

After this, the play was again submitted to the Lord Chamberlain. But, though beaten, he, too, understands the art of How Not To Do It. He licensed the play, but endorsed on his licence the condition that all the passages which implicated God in the history of Blanco Posnet must be omitted in representation. All the coarseness, the profligacy, the prostitution, the violence, the drinking-bar humor into which the light shines in the play are licensed, but the light itself is extinguished. I need hardly say that I have not availed myself of this licence, and do not intend to. There is enough licensed darkness in our theatres today without my adding to it.

AYOT ST LAWRENCE
14th July 1910

POSTSCRIPT. Since the above was written the Lord Chamberlain has made an attempt to evade his responsibility and perhaps to postpone his doom by appointing an advisory committee, unknown to the law, on which he will presumably throw any odium that may attach to refusals of licences in the future. This strange and lawless body will hardly reassure our moralists, who object much more to the plays he licenses than to those he suppresses, and are therefore unmoved by his plea that his refusals are few and far between. It consists of two eminent actors (one retired), an Oxford professor of literature, and two eminent barristers. As their assembly is neither created by statute nor sanctioned by custom, it is difficult to know what to call it until it advises the Lord Chamberlain to deprive some author of his means of livelihood, when it will, I presume, become a conspiracy, and be indictable accordingly; unless, indeed, it can persuade the Courts to recognize it as a new Estate of the Realm, created by the Lord Chamberlain. This constitutional position is so questionable that I strongly advise the members to resign promptly before the Lord Chamberlain gets them into trouble.

A number of women are sitting together in a big room not unlike an old English tithe barn in its timbered construction, but with windows high up next the roof. It is furnished as a courthouse, with the floor raised next the walls, and on this raised flooring a seat for the Sheriff, a rough jury box on his right, and a bar to put prisoners to on his left. In the well in the middle is a table with benches round it. A few other benches are in disorder round the room. The autumn sun is shining warmly through the windows and the open door. The women, whose dress and speech are those of pioneers of civilization in a territory of the United States of America, are seated round the table and on the benches, shucking nuts. The conversation is at its height.

BABSY [*a bumptious young slattern, with some good looks*] I say that a man that would steal a horse would do anything.

LOTTIE [*a sentimental girl, neat and clean*] Well, I never should look at it in that way. I do think killing a man is worse any day than stealing a horse.

HANNAH [*elderly and wise*] I dont say it's right to kill a man. In a place like this, where every man has to have a revolver, and where theres so much to try people's tempers, the men get to be a deal too free with one another in the way of shooting. God knows it's hard enough to have to bring a boy into the world and nurse him up to be a man only to have him brought home to you on a shutter, perhaps for nothing, or only just to shew that the man that killed him wasnt afraid of him. But men are like children when they get a gun in their hands: theyre not content til theyve used it on somebody.

JESSIE [*a good-natured but sharp-tongued, hoity-toity young woman; Babsy's rival in good looks and her superior in tidiness*] They shoot for the love of it. Look at them at a lynching. Theyre not content to hang the man; but directly the poor creature is swung up they all shoot him full of holes, wasting their cartridges that cost solid money, and pretending they do it in horror of his wickedness, though half of them would have a rope round their own necks if all they did was known. Let alone the mess it makes.

LOTTIE. I wish we could get more civilized. I dont like all this lynching and shooting. I dont believe any of us like it, if the truth were known.

BABSY. Our Sheriff is a real strong man. You want a strong man for a rough lot like our people here. He aint afraid to shoot and he aint afraid to hang. Lucky for us quiet ones, too.

JESSIE. Oh, dont talk to me. I know what men are. Of course he aint afraid to shoot and he aint afraid to hang. Wheres the risk in that with the law on his side and the whole crowd at his back longing for the lynching as if it was a spree? Would one of them own to it or let him own to it if they lynched the wrong man? Not them. What they call justice in this place is nothing but a breaking out of the devil thats in all of us. What I want to see is a Sheriff that aint afraid not to shoot and not to hang.

EMMA [*a sneak who sides with Babsy or Jessie, according to the fortune of war*] Well, I must say it does sicken me to see Sheriff Kemp putting down his foot, as he calls it. Why dont he put it down on his wife? She wants it worse than half the men he lynches. He and his Vigilance Committee, indeed!

BABSY [*incensed*] Oh, well! if people are going to take the part of horse-thieves against the Sheriff – ?

JESSIE. Who's taking the part of horse-thieves against the Sheriff?

BABSY. You are. Waitle your own horse is stolen, and youll know better. I had an uncle that died of thirst in the sage brush because a negro stole his horse. But they caught him and burned him; and serve him right, too.

EMMA. I have known a child that was born crooked because its mother had to do a horse's work that was stolen.

BABSY. There! You hear that? I say stealing a horse is ten times worse than killing a man. And if the Vigilance Committee ever gets hold of you, youd better have killed twenty men than as much as stole a saddle or bridle, much less a horse.

Elder Daniels comes in.

ELDER DANIELS. Sorry to disturb you, ladies; but the Vigilance Committee has taken a prisoner, and they want the room to try him in.

JESSIE. But they cant try him til Sheriff Kemp comes back from the wharf.

ELDER DANIELS. Yes; but we have to keep the prisoner here til he comes.

BABSY. What do you want to put him here for? Cant you tie him up in the Sheriff's stable?

ELDER DANIELS. He has a soul to be saved, almost like the rest of us. I am bound to try to put some religion into him before he goes into his Maker's presence after the trial.

HANNAH. What has he done, Mr Daniels?

ELDER DANIELS. Stole a horse.

BABSY. And are we to be turned out of the town hall for a horse-thief? Aint a stable good enough for his religion?

ELDER DANIELS. It may be good enough for his, Babsy; but, by your leave, it is not good enough for mine. While I am Elder here, I shall umbly endeavor to keep up the dignity of Him I serve to the best of my small ability. So I must ask you to be good enough to clear out. Allow me. [*He takes the sack of husks and puts it out of the way against the panels of the jury box*].

THE WOMEN [*murmuring*] Thats always the way. Just as we'd settled down to work. What harm are we doing? Well, it is tiresome. Let them finish the job themselves. Oh dear, oh dear! We cant have a minute to ourselves. Shoving us out like that!

HANNAH. Whose horse was it, Mr Daniels?

ELDER DANIELS [*returning to move the other sack*] I am sorry to say it was the Sheriff's horse – the one he loaned to young Strapper. Strapper loaned it to me; and the thief stole it, thinking it was mine. If it had been mine, I'd have forgiven him cheerfully. I'm sure I hoped he would get away; for he had two hours start of the Vigilance Committee. But they caught him. [*He disposes of the other sack also*].

JESSIE. It cant have been much of a horse if they caught him with two hours start.

ELDER DANIELS [*coming back to the centre of the group*] The strange thing is that he wasnt on the horse when they took him. He was walking; and of course he denies that he ever had the horse. The Sheriff's brother wanted to tie him up and lash him til he confessed what he'd done with it; but I couldnt allow that: it's not the law.

BABSY. Law! What right has a horse-thief to any law? Law is thrown away on a brute like that.

ELDER DANIELS. Dont say that, Babsy. No man should be made to confess by cruelty until religion has been tried and failed. Please God I'll get the whereabouts of the horse from him if youll be so good as to clear out from this. [*Disturbance*]. They are bringing him in. Now ladies! please, please.

They rise reluctantly. Hannah, Jessie, and Lottie retreat to the Sheriff's bench, shepherded by Daniels; but the other women crowd forward behind Babsy and Emma to see the prisoner.

Blanco Posnet is brought in by Strapper Kemp, the Sheriff's brother, and a cross-eyed man called Squinty. Others follow. Blanco is evidently a blackguard. It would be necessary to clean him to make a close guess at his age; but he is under forty, and an upturned, red moustache, and the arrangement of his hair in a crest on his brow, proclaim the dandy in spite of his intense disreputableness. He carries his head high, and has a fairly resolute mouth, though the fire of incipient delirium tremens is in his eye.

His arms are bound with a rope with a long end, which Squinty holds. They release him when he enters; and he stretches himself and lounges across the courthouse in front of the women. Strapper and the men remain between him and the door.

BABSY [*spitting at him as he passes her*] Horse-thief! horse-thief!

OTHERS. You will hang for it; do you hear? And serve you right. Serve you right. That will teach you. I wouldnt wait to try you. Lynch him straight off, the varmint. Yes, yes. Tell the boys. Lynch him.

BLANCO [*mocking*] 'Angels ever bright and fair –'

BABSY. You call me an angel, and I'll smack your dirty face for you.

BLANCO. 'Take, oh take me to your care.'

EMMA. There wont be any angels where youre going to.

OTHERS. Aha! Devils, more likely. And too good company for a horse-thief.

ALL. Horse-thief! Horse-thief! Horse-thief!

BLANCO. Do women make the law here, or men? Drive these heifers out.

THE WOMEN. Oh! [*They rush at him, vituperating, screaming passionately, tearing at him. Lottie puts her fingers in her ears and runs out. Hannah follows, shaking her head. Blanco is thrown down*]. Oh, did you hear what he called us? You foul-mouthed brute! You liar! How dare you put such a name to a decent woman? Let me get at him. You coward! Oh, he struck me: did you see that? Lynch him! Pete, will you stand by and hear me called names by a skunk like that? Burn him: burn him! Thats what I'd do with him. Aye, burn him!

THE MEN [*pulling the women away from Blanco, and getting them out partly by violence and partly by coaxing*] Here! come out of this. Let him alone. Clear the courthouse. Come on now. Out with you. Now, Sally: out you go. Let go my hair, or I'll twist your arm out. Ah, would you? Now, then: get along. You know you must go. Whats the use of scratching like that? Now, ladies, ladies, ladies. How would you like it if you were going to be hanged?

At last the women are pushed out, leaving Elder Daniels, the Sheriff's brother Strapper Kemp, and a few others with Blanco. Strapper is a lad just turning into a man: strong, selfish, sulky, and determined.

BLANCO [*sitting up and tidying himself*] –

Oh woman, in our hours of ease,
Uncertain, coy, and hard to please –

Is my face scratched? I can feel their damned claws all over me still. Am I bleeding? [*He sits on the nearest bench*].

ELDER DANIELS. Nothing to hurt. Theyve drawn a drop or two under your left eye.

STRAPPER. Lucky for you to have an eye left in your head.

BLANCO [*wiping the blood off*] –

When pain and anguish wring the brow,
A ministering angel thou.

Go out to them, Strapper Kemp; and tell them about your big brother's little horse that some wicked man stole. Go and cry in your mammy's lap.

STRAPPER [*furious*] You jounce me any more about that horse, Blanco Posnet; and I'll – I'll –

BLANCO. Youll scratch my face, wont you? Yah! Your brother's the Sheriff, aint he?

STRAPPER. Yes, he is. He hangs horse-thieves.

BLANCO [*with calm conviction*] He's a rotten Sheriff. Oh, a rotten Sheriff. If he did his first duty he'd hang himself. This is a rotten town. Your fathers came here on a false alarm of gold-digging; and when the gold didnt pan out, they lived by licking their young into habits of honest industry.

STRAPPER. If I hadnt promised Elder Daniels here to give him a chance to keep you out of Hell, I'd take the job of twisting your neck off the hands of the Vigilance Committee.

BLANCO [*with infinite scorn*] You and your rotten Elder, and your rotten Vigilance Committee!

STRAPPER. Theyre sound enough to hang a horse-thief, anyhow.

BLANCO. Any fool can hang the wisest man in the country. Nothing he likes better. But you cant hang me.

STRAPPER. Cant we?

BLANCO. No, you cant. I left the town this morning before sunrise, because it's a rotten town, and I couldnt bear to see it in the light. Your brother's horse did the same, as any sensible horse would. Instead of going to look for the horse, you went looking for me. That was a rotten thing to do, because the horse belonged to your brother – or to the man he stole it from – and I dont belong to him. Well, you found me; but you didnt find the horse. If I had took the horse, I'd have been on the horse. Would I have taken all that time to get to where I did if I'd a horse to carry me?

STRAPPER. I dont believe you started not for two hours after you say you did.

BLANCO. Who cares what you believe or dont believe? Is a man worth six of you to be hanged because youve lost your big brother's horse, and youll want to kill somebody to relieve your rotten feelings when he licks you for it? Not likely. Til you can find a witness that saw me with that horse you cant touch me; and you know it.

STRAPPER. Is that the law, Elder?

ELDER DANIELS. The Sheriff knows the law. I wouldnt say for sure; but I think it would be more seemly to have a witness. Go and round one up, Strapper; and leave me here alone to wrestle with his poor blinded soul.

STRAPPER. I'll get a witness all right enough. I know the road he took; and I'll ask at every house within sight of it for a mile out. Come, boys.

Strapper goes out with the others, leaving Blanco and Elder Daniels together. Blanco rises and strolls over to the Elder, surveying him with extreme disparagement.

BLANCO. Well, brother? Well, Boozy Posnet, alias Elder Daniels? Well, thief? Well, drunkard?

ELDER DANIELS. It's no good, Blanco. Theyll never believe we're brothers.

BLANCO. Never fear. Do you suppose I want to claim you? Do you suppose I'm proud of you? Youre a rotten brother, Boozy Posnet. All you ever did when I owned you was to borrow money from me to get drunk with. Now you lend money and sell drink to other people. I was ashamed of you before; and I'm worse ashamed of you now. I wont have you for a brother. Heaven gave you to me; but I return the blessing without thanks. So be easy: I shant blab. [*He turns his back on him and sits down*].

ELDER DANIELS. I tell you they wouldnt believe you; so what does it matter to me whether you blab or not? Talk sense, Blanco: theres no time for your foolery now; for youll be a dead man an hour after the Sheriff comes back. What possessed you to steal that horse?

BLANCO. I didnt steal it. I distrained on it for what you owed me. I thought it was yours. I was a fool to think that you owned anything but other people's property. You laid your hands on everything father and mother had when they died. I never asked you for a fair share. I never asked you for all the money I'd lent you from time to time. I asked you for mother's old necklace with the hair locket in it. You wouldnt give me that: you wouldnt give me anything. So as you refused me my due I took it, just to give you a lesson.

ELDER DANIELS. Why didnt you take the necklace if you must steal something? They wouldnt have hanged you for that.

BLANCO. Perhaps I'd rather be hanged for stealing a horse than let off for a damned piece of sentimentality.

ELDER DANIELS. Oh, Blanco, Blanco: spiritual pride has been your ruin. If youd only done like me, youd be a free and respectable man this day instead of laying there with a rope round your neck.

BLANCO [*turning on him*] Done like you! What do you mean? Drink like you, eh? Well, Ive done some of that lately. I see things.

ELDER DANIELS. Too late, Blanco: too late. [*Convulsively*] Oh, why didnt you drink as I used to? Why didnt you drink as I was led to by the Lord for my good, until the time came for me to give it up? It was drink that saved my character when I was a young man; and it was the want of it that spoiled yours. Tell me this. Did I ever get drunk when I was working?

BLANCO. No; but then you never worked when you had money enough to get drunk.

ELDER DANIELS. That just shews the wisdom of Providence and the Lord's mercy. God fulfils Himself in many ways: ways we little think of when we try to set up our own shortsighted laws against His Word. When does the Devil catch hold of a man? Not when he's working and not when he's drunk; but when he's idle and sober. Our own natures tell us to drink when we have nothing else to do. Look at you and me! When we'd both earned a pocketful of money, what did we do? Went on the spree, naturally. But I was humble minded. I did as the rest did. I gave my money in at the drink-shop; and I said, 'Fire me out when I have drunk it all up.' Did you ever see me sober while it lasted?

BLANCO. No; and you looked so disgusting that I wonder it didnt set me against drink for the rest of my life.

ELDER DANIELS. That was your spiritual pride, Blanco. You never reflected that when I was drunk I was in a state of innocence. Temptations and bad company and evil thoughts passed by me like the summer wind as you might say: I was too drunk to notice them. When the money was gone, and they fired me out, I was fired out like gold out of the furnace, with my character unspoiled and unspotted; and when I went back to work, the work kept me steady. Can you say as much, Blanco? Did *your* holidays leave *your* character unspoiled? Oh, no, no. It was theatres: it was gambling: it was evil company: it was reading vain romances: it was women, Blanco, women: it was wrong thoughts and gnawing discontent. It ended in your becoming a rambler and a gambler: it is going to end this evening on the gallows tree. Oh, what a lesson against spiritual pride! Oh, what a – [*Blanco throws his hat at him*].

BLANCO. Stow it, Boozy. Sling it. Cut it. Cheese it. Shut up. 'Shake not the dying sinner's sand.'

ELDER DANIELS. Aye: there you go, with your scraps of lustful poetry. But you cant deny what I tell you. Why, do you think I would put my soul in peril by selling drink if I thought it did no good, as them silly temperance reformers make out, flying in the face of the natural tastes implanted in us all for a good purpose? Not if I was to starve for it tomorrow. But I know better. I tell you, Blanco, what keeps America today the purest of the nations is that when she's not working she's too drunk to hear the voice of the tempter.

BLANCO. Dont deceive yourself, Boozy. You sell drink because you make a bigger profit out of it than you can by selling tea. And you gave up drink yourself because when you got that fit at Edwardstown the doctor told you youd die the next time; and that frightened you off it.

ELDER DANIELS [*fervently*] Oh thank God selling drink pays me! And thank God He sent me that fit as a warning that my drinking time was past and gone, and that He needed me for another service!

BLANCO. Take care, Boozy. He hasnt finished with you yet. He always has a trick up His sleeve –

ELDER DANIELS. Oh, is that the way to speak of the ruler of the universe – the great and almighty God?

BLANCO. He's a sly one. He's a mean one. He lies low for you. He plays cat and mouse with you. He lets you run loose until you think youre shut of Him; and then, when you least expect it, He's got you.

ELDER DANIELS. Speak more respectful, Blanco – more reverent.

BLANCO [*springing up and coming at him*] Reverent! Who taught you your reverent cant? Not your Bible. It says He cometh like a thief in the night – aye, like a thief – a horse-thief –

ELDER DANIELS [*shocked*] Oh!

BLANCO [*overbearing him*] And it's true. Thats how He caught me and put my neck into the halter. To spite me because I had no use for Him – because I lived my own life in my own way, and would have no truck with His 'Dont do this,' and 'You mustnt do that,' and 'Youll go to Hell if you do the other.' I gave Him the go-bye and did without Him all these years. But He caught me out at last. The laugh is with Him as far as hanging me goes.

[*He thrusts his hands into his pockets and lounges moodily away from Daniels, to the table, where he sits facing the jury box*].

ELDER DANIELS. Dont dare to put your theft on Him, man. It was the Devil tempted you to steal the horse.

BLANCO. Not a bit of it. Neither God nor Devil tempted me to take the horse: I took it on my own. He had a cleverer trick than that ready for me. [*He takes his hands out of his pockets and clenches his fists*]. Gosh! When I think that I might have been safe and fifty miles away by now with that horse; and here I am waiting to be hung up and filled with lead! What came to me? What made me such a fool? Thats what I want to know. Thats the great secret.

ELDER DANIELS [*at the opposite side of the table*] Blanco: the great secret now is, what did you do with the horse?

BLANCO [*striking the table with his fist*] May my lips be blighted like my soul if ever I tell that to you or any mortal man! They may roast me alive or cut me to ribbons; but Strapper Kemp shall never have the laugh on me over that job. Let them hang me. Let them shoot. So long as they are shooting a man and not a snivelling skunk and softy, I can stand up to them and take all they can give me – game.

ELDER DANIELS. Dont be headstrong, Blanco. Whats the use? [*Slyly*] They might let up on you if you put Strapper in the way of getting his brother's horse back.

BLANCO. Not they. Hanging's too big a treat for them to give up a fair chance. Ive done it myself. Ive yelled with the dirtiest of them when a man no worse than myself was swung up. Ive emptied my revolver into him, and persuaded myself that he deserved it and that I was doing justice with strong stern men. Well, my turn's come now. Let the men I yelled at and shot at look up out of Hell and see the boys yelling and shooting at me as *I* swing up.

ELDER DANIELS. Well, even if you want to be hanged, is that any reason why Strapper shouldnt have his horse? I tell you I'm responsible to him for it. [*Bending over the table and coaxing him*]. Act like a brother, Blanco: tell me what you done with it.

BLANCO [*shortly, getting up and leaving the table*] Never you mind what I done with it. I was done out of it: let that be enough for you.

ELDER DANIELS [*following him*] Then why dont you put us on to the man that done you out of it?

BLANCO. Because he'd be too clever for you, just as he was too clever for me.

ELDER DANIELS. Make your mind easy about that, Blanco. He wont be too clever for the boys and Sheriff Kemp if you put them on his trail.

BLANCO. Yes, he will. It wasnt a man.

ELDER DANIELS. Then what was it?

BLANCO [*pointing upward*] Him.

ELDER DANIELS. Oh what a way to utter His holy name!

BLANCO. He done me out of it. He meant to pay off old scores by bringing me here. He means to win the deal and you cant stop Him. Well, He's made a fool of me; but He cant frighten me. I'm not going to beg off. I'll fight off if I get a chance. I'll lie off if they cant get a witness against me. But back down I never will, not if all the hosts of heaven come to snivel at me in white surplices and offer me my life in exchange for an umble and a contrite heart.

ELDER DANIELS. Youre not in your right mind, Blanco. I'll tell em youre mad. I believe theyll let you off on that. [*He makes for the door*].

BLANCO [*seizing him, with horror in his eyes*] Dont go: dont leave me alone: do you hear?

ELDER DANIELS. Has your conscience brought you to this that youre afraid to be left alone in broad daylight, like a child in the dark.

BLANCO. I'm afraid of Him and His tricks. When I have you to raise the devil in me – when I have people to shew off before and keep me game, I'm all right; but Ive lost my nerve for being alone since this morning. It's when youre alone that He takes His advantage. He might turn my head again. He might send people to me – not real people perhaps. [*Shivering*] By God, I dont believe that woman and the child were real. I dont. I never noticed them til they were at my elbow.

ELDER DANIELS. What woman and what child? What are you talking about? Have you been drinking too hard?

BLANCO. Never you mind. Youve got to stay with me: thats all; or else send someone else – someone rottener than yourself to keep the devil in me. Strapper Kemp will do. Or a few of those scratching devils of women.

Strapper Kemp comes back.

ELDER DANIELS [*to Strapper*] He's gone off his head.

STRAPPER. Foxing, more likely. [*Going past Daniels and talking to Blanco nose to nose*]. It's no good: we hang madmen here; and a good job too!

BLANCO. I feel safe with you, Strapper. Youre one of the rottenest.

STRAPPER. You know youre done, and that you may as well be hanged for a sheep as a lamb. So talk away. Ive got my witness; and I'll trouble you not to make a move towards her when she comes in to identify you.

BLANCO [*retreating in terror*] A woman? She aint real: neither is the child.

ELDER DANIELS. He's raving about a woman and a child. I tell you he's gone off his chump.

STRAPPER [*calling to those without*] Shew the lady in there.

Feemy Evans comes in. She is a young woman of 23 or 24, with impudent manners, battered good looks, and dirty-fine dress.

ELDER DANIELS. Morning, Feemy.

FEEMY. Morning, Elder. [*She passes on and slips her arm familiarly through Strapper's*].

STRAPPER. Ever see him before, Feemy?

FEEMY. Thats the little lot that was on your horse this morning, Strapper. Not a doubt of it.

BLANCO [*implacably contemptuous*] Go home and wash yourself, you slut.

FEEMY [*reddening and disengaging her arm from Strapper's*] I'm clean enough to hang you, anyway. [*Going over to him threateningly*]. Youre no true American man, to insult a woman like that.

BLANCO. A woman! Oh Lord! You saw me on a horse, did you?

FEEMY. Yes, I did.

BLANCO. Got up early on purpose to do it, didnt you?

FEEMY. No I didnt: I stayed up late on a spree.

BLANCO. I was on a horse, was I?

FEEMY. Yes you were; and if you deny it youre a liar.

BLANCO [*to Strapper*] She saw a man on a horse when she was too drunk to tell which was the man and which was the horse –

FEEMY [*breaking in*] You lie. I wasnt drunk – at least not as drunk as that.

BLANCO [*ignoring the interruption*] – and you found a man without a horse. Is a man on a horse the same as a man on foot? Yah! Take your witness away. Who's going to believe her? Throw her out on the dump. Youve got to find that horse before you get a rope round my neck. [*He turns away from her contemptuously, and sits at the table with his back to the jury box*].

FEEMY [*following him*] I'll hang you, you dirty horse-thief; or not a man in this camp will ever get a word or a look from me again. Youre just trash: thats what you are. White trash.

BLANCO. And what are you, darling? What are you? Youre a worse danger to a town like this than ten horse-thieves.

FEEMY. Mr Kemp: will you stand by and hear me insulted in that low way? [*To Blanco, spitefully*] I'll see you swung up and I'll see you cut down: I'll see you high and I'll see you low, as dangerous as I am. [*He laughs*]. Oh you neednt try to brazen it out. Youll look white enough before the boys are done with you.

BLANCO. You do me good, Feemy. Stay by me to the end, wont you? Hold my hand to the last; and I'll die game. [*He puts out his hand: she strikes savagely at it; but he withdraws it in time and laughs at her discomfiture*].

FEEMY. You –

ELDER DANIELS. Never mind him, Feemy: he's not right in his head today. [*She receives the assurance with contemptuous incredulity, and sits down on the step of the Sheriff's dais*].

Sheriff Kemp comes in: a stout man, with large flat ears, and a neck thicker than his head.

ELDER DANIELS. Morning, Sheriff.

THE SHERIFF. Morning, Elder. [*Passing on*]. Morning, Strapper. [*Passing on*]. Morning, Miss Evans. [*Stopping between Strapper and Blanco*]. Is this the prisoner?

BLANCO [*rising*] Thats so. Morning, Sheriff.

THE SHERIFF. Morning. You know, I suppose, that if youve stole a horse and the jury find against you, you wont have any time to settle your affairs. Consequently, if you feel guilty, youd better settle em now.

BLANCO. Affairs be damned! Ive got none.

THE SHERIFF. Well, are you in a proper state of mind? Has the Elder talked to you?

BLANCO. He has. And I say it's against the law. It's torture: thats what it is.

ELDER DANIELS. He's not accountable. He's out of his mind, Sheriff. He's not fit to go into the presence of his Maker.

THE SHERIFF. You are a merciful man, Elder; but you wont take the boys with you there. [*To Blanco*] If it comes to hanging you, youd better for your own sake be hanged in a proper state of mind than in an improper one. But it wont make any difference to us: make no mistake about that.

BLANCO. Lord keep me wicked til I die! Now Ive said my little prayer. I'm ready. Not that I'm guilty, mind you; but this is a rotten town, dead certain to do the wrong thing.

THE SHERIFF. You wont be asked to live long in it, I guess. [*To Strapper*] Got the witness all right, Strapper?

STRAPPER. Yes, got everything.

BLANCO. Except the horse.

THE SHERIFF. Whats that? Aint you got the horse?

STRAPPER. No. He traded it before we overtook him, I guess. But Feemy saw him on it.

FEEMY. She did.

STRAPPER. Shall I call in the boys?

BLANCO. Just a moment, Sheriff. A good appearance is everything in a low-class place like this. [*He takes out a pocket comb and mirror, and retires towards the dais to arrange his hair*].

ELDER DANIELS. Oh, think of your immortal soul, man, not of your foolish face.

BLANCO. I cant change my soul, Elder: it changes me – sometimes. Feemy: I'm too pale. Let me rub my cheek against yours, darling.

FEEMY. You lie: my color's my own, such as it is. And a pretty color youll be when youre hung white and shot red.

BLANCO. Aint she spiteful, Sheriff?

THE SHERIFF. Time's wasted on you. [*To Strapper*] Go and see if the boys are ready. Some of them were short of cartridges, and went down to the store to buy them. They may as well have their fun; and itll be shorter for him.

STRAPPER. Young Jack has brought a boxful up. Theyre all ready.

THE SHERIFF [*going to the dais and addressing Blanco*] Your place is at the bar there. Take it. [*Blanco bows ironically and goes to the bar*]. Miss Evans: youd best sit at the table. [*She does so, at the corner nearest the bar. The Elder takes the opposite corner. The Sheriff takes his chair*]. All ready, Strapper.

STRAPPER [*at the door*] All in to begin.

The crowd comes in and fills the court. Babsy, Jessie, and Emma come to the Sheriff's right; Hannah and Lottie to his left.

THE SHERIFF. Silence there. The jury will take their places as usual. [*They do so*].

BLANCO. I challenge this jury, Sheriff.

THE FOREMAN. Do you, by Gosh?

THE SHERIFF. On what ground?

BLANCO. On the general ground that it's a rotten jury. [*Laughter*].

THE SHERIFF. Thats not a lawful ground of challenge.

THE FOREMAN. It's a lawful ground for me to shoot yonder skunk at sight, first time I meet him, if he survives this trial.

BLANCO. I challenge the Foreman because he's prejudiced.

THE FOREMAN. I say you lie. We mean to hang you, Blanco Posnet; but you will be hanged fair.

THE JURY. Hear, hear!

STRAPPER [*to the Sheriff*] George: this is rot. How can you get an unprejudiced jury if the prisoner starts by telling them theyre all rotten? If theres any prejudice against him he has himself to thank for it.

THE BOYS. Thats so. Of course he has. Insulting the court! Challenge be jiggered! Gag him.

NESTOR [*a juryman with a long white beard, drunk, the oldest man present*] Besides, Sheriff, I go so far as to say that the man that is not prejudiced against a horse-thief is not fit to sit on a jury in this town.

THE BOYS. Right. Bully for you, Nestor! Thats the straight truth. Of course he aint. Hear, hear!

THE SHERIFF. That is no doubt true, old man. Still, you must get as unprejudiced as you can. The critter has a right to his chance, such as he is. So now go right ahead. If the prisoner dont like this jury, he should have stole a horse in another town; for this is all the jury he'll get here.

THE FOREMAN. Thats so, Blanco Posnet.

THE SHERIFF [*to Blanco*] Dont you be uneasy. You will get justice here. It may be rough justice; but it is justice.

BLANCO. What is justice?

THE SHERIFF. Hanging horse-thieves is justice; so now you know. Now then: weve wasted enough time. Hustle with your witness there, will you?

BLANCO [*indignantly bringing down his fist on the bar*] Swear the jury. A rotten Sheriff you are not to know that the jury's got to be sworn.

THE FOREMAN [*galled*] Be swore for you! Not likely. What do you say, old son?

NESTOR [*deliberately and solemnly*] I say: GUILTY!!!

THE BOYS [*tumultuously rushing at Blanco*] Thats it. Guilty, guilty. Take him out and hang him. He's found guilty. Fetch a rope. Up with him. [*They are about to drag him from the bar*].

THE SHERIFF [*rising, pistol in hand*] Hands off that man. Hands off him, I say, Squinty, or I drop you, and would if you were my own son. [*Dead silence*]. I'm Sheriff here; and it's for me to say when he may lawfully be hanged. [*They release him*].

BLANCO. As the actor says in the play, 'a Daniel come to judgment'. Rotten actor he was, too.

THE SHERIFF. Elder Daniels is come to judgment all right, my lad. Elder: the floor is yours. [*The Elder rises*]. Give your evidence. The truth and the whole truth and nothing but the truth, so help you God.

ELDER DANIELS. Sheriff: let me off this. I didnt ought to swear away this man's life. He and I are, in a manner of speaking, brothers.

THE SHERIFF. It does you credit, Elder: every man here will acknowledge it. But religion is one thing: law is another. In religion we're all brothers. In law we cut our brother off when he steals horses.

THE FOREMAN. Besides, you neednt hang him, you know. Theres

plenty of willing hands to take that job off your conscience. So rip ahead, old son.

STRAPPER. Youre accountable to me for the horse until you clear yourself, Elder: remember that.

BLANCO. Out with it, you fool.

ELDER DANIELS. You might own up, Blanco, as far as my evidence goes. Everybody knows I borrowed one of the Sheriff's horses from Strapper because my own's gone lame. Everybody knows you arrived in the town yesterday and put up in my house. Everybody knows that in the morning the horse was gone and you were gone.

BLANCO [*in a forensic manner*] Sheriff: the Elder, though known to you and to all here as no brother of mine and the rottenest liar in this town, is speaking the truth for the first time in his life as far as what he says about me is concerned. As to the horse, I say nothing; except that it was the rottenest horse you ever tried to sell.

THE SHERIFF. How do you know it was a rotten horse if you didnt steal it?

BLANCO. I d o n t know of my own knowledge. I only argue that if the horse had been worth its keep, you wouldnt have lent it to Strapper, and Strapper wouldnt have lent it to this eloquent and venerable ram. [*Suppressed laughter*]. And now I ask him this. [*To the Elder*] Did we or did we not have a quarrel last evening about a certain article that was left by my mother, and that I considered I had a right to more than you? And did you say one word to me about the horse not belonging to you?

ELDER DANIELS. Why should I? We never said a word about the horse at all. How was I to know what it was in your mind to do?

BLANCO. Bear witness all that I had a right to take a horse from him without stealing to make up for what he denied me. I am no thief. But you havnt proved yet that I took the horse. Strapper Kemp: had I the horse when you took me or had I not?

STRAPPER. No, nor you hadnt a railway train neither. But Feemy Evans saw you pass on the horse at four o'clock twenty-five miles from the spot where I took you at seven on the road to Pony Harbor. Did you walk twenty-five miles in three hours? That so, Feemy? eh?

FEEMY. Thats so. At four I saw him. [*To Blanco*] Thats done for you.

THE SHERIFF. You say you saw him on my horse?

FEEMY. I did.

BLANCO. And I ate it, I suppose, before Strapper fetched up with me. [*Suddenly and dramatically*] Sheriff: I accuse Feemy of immoral relations with Strapper.

FEEMY. Oh you liar!

BLANCO. I accuse the fair Euphemia of immoral relations with every man in this town, including yourself, Sheriff. I say this is a conspiracy to kill me between Feemy and Strapper because I wouldnt touch Feemy with a pair of tongs. I say you darent hang any white man on the word of a woman of bad character. I stand on the honor and virtue of my American manhood. I say that she's not had the oath, and that you darent for the honor of the town give her the oath because her lips would blaspheme the holy Bible if they touched it. I say thats the law; and if you are a proper United States Sheriff and not a low-down lyncher, youll hold up the law and not let it be dragged in the mud by your brother's kept woman.

Great excitement among the women. The men much puzzled.

JESSIE. Thats right. She didnt ought to be let kiss the Book.

EMMA. How could the like of her tell the truth?

BABSY. It would be an insult to every respectable woman here to believe her.

FEEMY. It's easy to be respectable with nobody ever offering you a chance to be anything else.

THE WOMEN [*clamoring all together*] Shut up, you hussy. Youre a disgrace. How dare you open your lips to answer your betters? Hold your tongue and learn your place, miss. You painted slut! Whip her out of the town!

THE SHERIFF. Silence, Do you hear. Silence. [*The clamor ceases*]. Did anyone else see the prisoner with the horse?

FEEMY [*passionately*] Aint I good enough?

BABSY. No. Youre dirt: thats what you are.

FEEMY. And you –

THE SHERIFF. Silence. This trial is a man's job; and if the women forget their sex they can go out or be put out. Strapper and Miss

Evans: you cant have it two ways. You can run straight, or you can run gay, so to speak; but you cant run both ways together. There is also a strong feeling among the men of this town that a line should be drawn between those that are straight wives and mothers and those that are, in the words of the Book of Books, taking the primrose path. We dont wish to be hard on any woman; and most of us have a personal regard for Miss Evans for the sake of old times; but theres no getting out of the fact that she has private reasons for wishing to oblige Strapper, and that – if she will excuse my saying so – she is not what I might call morally particular as to what she does to oblige him. Therefore I ask the prisoner not to drive us to give Miss Evans the oath. I ask him to tell us fair and square, as a man who has but a few minutes between him and eternity, what he done with my horse.

THE BOYS. Hear, hear! Thats right. Thats fair. That does it. Now, Blanco. Own up.

BLANCO. Sheriff: you touch me home. This is a rotten world; but there is still one thing in it that remains sacred even to the rottenest of us, and that is a horse.

THE BOYS. Good. Well said, Blanco. Thats straight.

BLANCO. You have a right to your horse, Sheriff; and if I could put you in the way of getting it back, I would. But if I had that horse I shouldnt be here. As I hope to be saved, Sheriff – or rather as I hope to be damned; for I have no taste for pious company and no talent for playing the harp – I know no more of that horse's whereabouts than you do yourself.

STRAPPER. Who did you trade him to?

BLANCO. I did not trade him. I got nothing for him or by him. I stand here with a rope round my neck for the want of him. When you took me, did I fight like a thief or run like a thief; and was there any sign of a horse on me or near me?

STRAPPER. You were looking at a rainbow like a damned silly fool instead of keeping your wits about you; and we stole up on you and had you tight before you could draw a bead on us.

THE SHERIFF. That dont sound like good sense. What would he look at a rainbow for?

BLANCO. I'll tell you, Sheriff. I was looking at it because there was something written on it.

SHERIFF. How do you mean written on it?

BLANCO. The words were, 'Ive got the cinch on you this time, Blanco Posnet.' Yes, Sheriff, I saw those words in green on the red streak of the rainbow; and as I saw them I felt Strapper's grab on my arm and Squinty's on my pistol.

THE FOREMAN. He's shammin mad: thats what he is. Aint it about time to give a verdict and have a bit of fun, Sheriff?

THE BOYS. Yes, lets have a verdict. We're wasting the whole afternoon. Cut it short.

THE SHERIFF [*making up his mind*] Swear Feemy Evans, Elder. She dont need to touch the Book. Let her say the words.

FEEMY. Worse people than me has kissed that Book. What wrong Ive done, most of you went shares in. Ive to live, havnt I? same as the rest of you. However, it makes no odds to me, I guess the truth is the truth and a lie is a lie, on the Book or off it.

BABSY. Do as youre told. Who are you, to be let talk about it?

THE SHERIFF. Silence there, I tell you. Sail ahead, Elder.

ELDER DANIELS. Feemy Evans: do you swear to tell the truth and the whole truth and nothing but the truth, so help you God.

FEEMY. I do, so help me –

SHERIFF. Thats enough. Now, on your oath, did you see the prisoner on my horse this morning on the road to Pony Harbor?

FEEMY. On my oath – [*Disturbance and crowding at the door*].

AT THE DOOR. Now then, now then! Where are you shovin to? Whats up? Order in court. Chuck him out. Silence. You cant come in here. Keep back.

Strapper rushes to the door and forces his way out.

SHERIFF [*savagely*] Whats this noise? Cant you keep quiet there? Is this a Sheriff's court or is it a saloon?

BLANCO. Dont interrupt a lady in the act of hanging a gentleman. Wheres your manners?

FEEMY. I'll hang you, Blanco Posnet. I will. I wouldnt [say] for fifty dollars I hadnt seen you this morning. I'll teach you to be civil to me next time, for all I'm not good enough to kiss the Book.

BLANCO. Lord keep me wicked till I die! I'm game for anything while youre spitting dirt at me, Feemy.

RENEWED TUMULT AT THE DOOR. Here, what's this? Fire them out. Not me. Who are you that I should get out of your way? Oh, stow it. Well, she cant come in. What woman? What horse? Whats the good of shoving like that? Who says? No! you dont say!

THE SHERIFF. Gentlemen of the Vigilance Committee: clear that doorway. Out with them in the name of the law.

STRAPPER [*without*] Hold hard, George. [*At the door*] Theyve got the horse. [*He comes in, followed by Waggoner Jo, an elderly carter, who crosses the court to the jury side. Strapper pushes his way to the Sheriff and speaks privately to him*].

THE BOYS. What! No! Got the horse! Sheriff's horse! Who took it, then? Where? Get out. Yes it is, sure. I tell you it is. It's the horse all right enough. Rot. Go and look. By Gum!

THE SHERIFF [*to Strapper*] You dont say!

STRAPPER. It's here, I tell you.

WAGGONER JO. It's here all right enough, Sheriff.

STRAPPER. And theyve got the thief too.

ELDER DANIELS. Then it aint Blanco.

STRAPPER. No: it's a woman. [*Blanco yells and covers his eyes with his hands*].

THE WHOLE CROWD. A woman!

THE SHERIFF. Well, fetch her in. [*Strapper goes out. The Sheriff continues, to Feemy*] And what do you mean, you lying jade, by putting up this story on us about Blanco?

FEEMY. I aint put up no story on you. This is a plant: you see if it isnt.

Strapper returns with a woman. Her expression of intense grief silences them as they crane over one another's heads to see her. Strapper takes her to the corner of the table. The Elder moves up to make room for her.

BLANCO [*terrified*] Sheriff: that woman aint real. You take care. That woman will make you do what you never intended. Thats the rainbow woman. Thats the woman that brought me to this.

THE SHERIFF. Shut your mouth, will you. Youve got the horrors. [*To the woman*] Now you. Who are you? and what are you doing with a horse that doesnt belong to you?

THE WOMAN. I took it to save my child's life. I thought it would get me to a doctor in time. The child was choking with croup.

BLANCO [*strangling, and trying to laugh*] A little choker: thats the word for him. His choking wasnt real: wait and see mine. [*He feels his neck with a sob*].

THE SHERIFF. Wheres the child?

STRAPPER. On Pug Jackson's bench in his shed. He's makin a coffin for it.

BLANCO [*with a horrible convulsion of the throat – frantically*] Dead! The little Judas kid! The child I gave my life for! [*He breaks into hideous laughter*].

THE SHERIFF [*jarred beyond endurance by the sound*] Hold your noise, will you. Shove his neckerchief into his mouth if he dont stop. [*To the woman*] Dont you mind him, maam: he's mad with drink and devilment. I suppose theres no fake about this, Strapper. Who found her?

WAGGONER JO. I did, Sheriff. Theres no fake about it. I came on her on the track round by Red Mountain. She was settin on the ground with the dead body on her lap, stupid-like. The horse was grazin on the other side o the road.

THE SHERIFF [*puzzled*] Well, this is blamed queer. [*To the woman*] What call had you to take the horse from Elder Daniels' stable to find a doctor? Theres a doctor in the very next house.

BLANCO [*mopping his dabbled red crest and trying to be ironically gay*] Story simply wont wash, my angel. You got it from the man that stole the horse. He gave it to you because he was a softy and went to bits when you played off the sick kid on him. Well, I guess that clears me. I'm not that sort. Catch me putting my neck in a noose for anybody's kid!

THE FOREMAN. Dont you go putting her up to what to say. She said she took it.

THE WOMAN. Yes: I took it from a man that met me. I thought God sent him to me. I rode here joyfully thinking so all the time to myself. Then I noticed that the child was like lead in my arms. God would never have been so cruel as to send me the horse to disappoint me like that.

BLANCO. Just what He would do.

STRAPPER. We aint got nothin to do with that. This is the man, aint he? [*pointing to Blanco*].

THE WOMAN [*pulling herself together after looking scaredly at Blanco, and then at the Sheriff and at the jury*] No.

THE FOREMAN. You lie.

THE SHERIFF. Youve got to tell us the truth. Thats the law, you know.

THE WOMAN. The man looked a bad man. He cursed me; and he cursed the child: God forgive him! But something came over him. I was desperate. I put the child in his arms; and it got its little fingers down his neck and called him Daddy and tried to kiss him; for it was not right in its head with the fever. He said it was a little Judas kid, and that it was betraying him with a kiss, and that he'd swing for it. And then he gave me the horse, and went away crying and laughing and singing dreadful dirty wicked words to hymn tunes like as if he had seven devils in him.

STRAPPER. She's lying. Give her the oath, George.

THE SHERIFF. Go easy there. Youre a smart boy, Strapper; but youre not Sheriff yet. This is my job. You just wait. I submit that we're in a difficulty here. If Blanco was the man, the lady cant, as a white woman, give him away. She oughtnt to be put in the position of having either to give him away or commit perjury. On the other hand, we dont want a horse-thief to get off through a lady's delicacy.

THE FOREMAN. No we dont; and we dont intend he shall. Not while I am foreman of this jury.

BLANCO [*with intense expression*] A rotten foreman! Oh, what a rotten foreman!

THE SHERIFF. Shut up, will you. Providence shews us a way out here. Two women saw Blanco with a horse. One has a delicacy about saying so. The other will excuse me saying that delicacy is not her strongest holt. She can give the necessary witness. Feemy Evans: youve taken the oath. You saw the man that took the horse.

FEEMY. I did. And he was a low-down rotten drunken lying hound that would go further to hurt a woman any day than to help her. And if he ever did a good action it was because he was too drunk to know what he was doing. So it's no harm to hang him. She said he cursed her and went away blaspheming and singing things that were not fit for the child to hear.

BLANCO [*troubled*] I didnt mean them for the child to hear, you venomous devil.

THE SHERIFF. All thats got nothing to do with us. The question you have to answer is, was that man Blanco Posnet?

THE WOMAN. No. I say no. I swear it. Sheriff: dont hang that man: oh dont. You may hang me instead if you like: Ive nothing to live for now. You darent take her word against mine. She never had a child: I can see it in her face.

FEEMY [*stung to the quick*] I can hang him in spite of you, anyhow. Much good your child is to you now, lying there on Pug Jackson's bench!

BLANCO [*rushing at her with a shriek*] I'll twist your heart out of you for that. [*They seize him before he can reach her*].

FEEMY [*mocking him as he struggles to get at her*] Ha, ha, Blanco Posnet. You cant touch me; and I can hang you. Ha, ha! Oh, I'll do for you. I'll twist your heart and I'll twist your neck [*He is dragged back to the bar and leans on it, gasping and exhausted*]. Give me the oath again, Elder. I'll settle him. And do you [*to the woman*] take your sickly face away from in front of me.

STRAPPER. Just turn your back on her there, will you?

THE WOMAN. God knows I dont want to see her commit murder. [*She folds her shawl over her head*].

THE SHERIFF. Now, Miss Evans: cut it short. Was the prisoner the man you saw this morning or was he not? Yes or no?

FEEMY [*a little hysterically*] I'll tell you fast enough. Dont think I'm a softy.

THE SHERIFF [*losing patience*] Here: weve had enough of this. You tell the truth, Feemy Evans; and let us have no more of your lip. Was the prisoner the man or was he not? On your oath?

FEEMY. On my oath and as I'm a living woman – [*flinching*] Oh God! he felt the little child's hands on his neck – I cant [*bursting into a flood of tears and scolding at the other woman*] It's you with your snivelling face that has put me off it. [*Desperately*] No: it wasnt him. I only said it out of spite because he insulted me. May I be struck dead if I ever saw him with the horse!

Everybody draws a long breath. Dead silence.

BLANCO [*whispering at her*] Softy! Cry-baby! Landed like me! Doing what you never intended! [*Taking up his hat and speaking in his ordinary tone*] I presume I may go now, Sheriff.

STRAPPER. Here, hold hard.

THE FOREMAN. Not if we know it, you dont.

THE BOYS [*barring the way to the door*] You stay where you are. Stop a bit, stop a bit. Dont you be in such a hurry. Dont let him go. Not much.

Blanco stands motionless, his eyes fixed, thinking hard, and apparently deaf to what is going on.

THE SHERIFF [*rising solemnly*] Silence there. Wait a bit. I take it that if the Sheriff is satisfied and the owner of the horse is satisfied, theres no more to be said. I have had to remark on former occasions that what is wrong with this court is that theres too many Sheriffs in it. Today there is going to be one, and only one; and that one is your humble servant. I call that to the notice of the Foreman of the jury, and also to the notice of young Strapper. I am also the owner of the horse. Does any man say I am not? [*Silence*]. Very well, then. In my opinion, to commandeer a horse for the purpose of getting a dying child to a doctor is not stealing, provided, as in the present case, that the horse is returned safe and sound. I rule that there has been no theft.

NESTOR. That aint the law.

THE SHERIFF. I fine you a dollar for contempt of court, and will collect it myself off you as you leave the building. And as the boys have been disappointed of their natural sport, I shall give them a little fun by standing outside the door and taking up a collection for the bereaved mother of the late kid that shewed up Blanco Posnet.

THE BOYS. A collection. Oh, I say! Calls that sport? Is this a mothers' meeting? Well, I'll be jiggered! Where does the sport come in?

THE SHERIFF [*continuing*] The sport comes in, my friends, not so much in contributing as in seeing others fork out. Thus each contributes to the general enjoyment; and all contribute to his. Blanco Posnet: you go free under the protection of the Vigilance Committee for just long enough to get you out of this town, which is not a healthy place for you. As you are in a hurry, I'll sell you the horse at a reasonable figure. Now, boys, let nobody go out till I get to the door. The court is adjourned. [*He goes out*].

STRAPPER [*to Feemy, as he goes to the door*] I'm done with you. Do you hear? I'm done with you. [*He goes out sulkily*].

FEEMY [*calling after him*] As if I cared about a stingy brat like you! Go back to the freckled maypole you left for me: youve been fretting for her long enough.

THE FOREMAN [*to Blanco, on his way out*] A man like you makes me sick. Just sick. [*Blanco makes no sign. The Foreman spits disgustedly, and follows Strapper out. The Jurymen leave the box, except Nestor, who collapses in a drunken sleep*].

BLANCO [*suddenly rushing from the bar to the table and jumping up on it*] Boys, I'm going to preach you a sermon on the moral of this day's proceedings.

THE BOYS [*crowding round him*] Yes: lets have a sermon. Go ahead, Blanco. Silence for Elder Blanco. Tune the organ. Let us pray.

NESTOR [*staggering out of his sleep*] Never hold up your head in this town again. I'm done with you.

BLANCO [*pointing inexorably to Nestor*] Drunk in church. Disturbing the preacher. Hand him out.

THE BOYS [*chivying Nestor out*] Now, Nestor, outside. Outside, Nestor. Out you go. Get your subscription ready for the Sheriff. Skiddoo, Nestor.

NESTOR. Afraid to be hanged! Afraid to be hanged! [*At the door*] Coward! [*He is thrown out*].

BLANCO. Dearly beloved brethren –

A BOY. Same to you, Blanco. [*Laughter*].

BLANCO. And many of them. Boys: this is a rotten world.

ANOTHER BOY. Lord have mercy on us, miserable sinners. [*More laughter*].

BLANCO [*forcibly*] No: thats where youre wrong. Dont flatter yourselves that youre miserable sinners. Am I a miserable sinner? No: I'm a fraud and a failure. I started in to be a bad man like the rest of you. You all started in to be bad men or you wouldnt be in this jumped-up, jerked-off, hospital-turned-out camp that calls itself a town. I took the broad path because I thought I was a man and not a snivelling canting turning-the-other-cheek apprentice angel serving his time in a vale of tears. They talked Christianity to us on Sundays; but when they really meant business they told us never to take a blow without giving it back, and to get dollars. When they talked the golden rule to me, I just looked at them as if they werent there, and spat. But when they told me to try to live my life so that I could always look my fellowman straight in the eye and tell him to go to hell, that fetched me.

THE BOYS. Quite right. Good. Bully for you, Blanco, old son. Right good sense too. Aha-a-ah!

BLANCO. Yes: but whats come of it all? Am I a real bad man? a man of game and grit? a man that does what he likes and goes over or through other people to his own gain? or am I a snivelling cry-baby that let a horse his life depended on be took from him by a woman, and then sat on the grass looking at the rainbow and let himself be took like a hare in a trap by Strapper Kemp: a lad whose back I or any grown man here could break against his knee? I'm a rottener fraud and failure than the Elder here. And youre all as rotten as me, or youd have lynched me.

A BOY. Anything to oblige you, Blanco.

ANOTHER. We can do it yet if you feel really bad about it.

BLANCO. No: the devil's gone out of you. We're all frauds. Theres none of us real good and none of us real bad.

ELDER DANIELS. There is One above, Blanco.

BLANCO. What do you know about Him? you that always talk as if He never did anything without asking your rotten leave first? Why did the child die? Tell me that if you can. He cant have wanted to kill the child. Why did He make me go soft on the child if He was going hard on it Himself? Why should He go hard on the innocent kid and go soft on a rotten thing like me? Why did I go soft myself? Why did the Sheriff go soft? Why did Feemy go soft? Whats this game that upsets our game? For seems to me theres two games bein played. Our game is a rotten game that makes me feel I'm dirt and that youre all as rotten dirt as me. T'other game may be a silly game; but it aint rotten. When the Sheriff played it he stopped being rotten. When Feemy played it the paint nearly dropped off her face. When I played it I cursed myself for a fool; but I lost the rotten feel all the same.

ELDER DANIELS. It was the Lord speaking to your soul, Blanco.

BLANCO. Oh yes: you know all about the Lord, dont you? Youre in the Lord's confidence. He wouldnt for the world do anything to shock you, would He, Boozy dear? Yah! What about the croup?

It was early days when He made the croup, I guess. It was the best He could think of then; but when it turned out wrong on His hands He made you and me to fight the croup for Him. You bet He didnt make us for nothing; and He wouldnt have made us at all if He could have done His work without us. By Gum, that must be what we're for! He'd never have made us to be rotten drunken blackguards like me, and good-for-nothing rips like Feemy. He made me because He had a job for me. He let me run loose til the job was ready; and then I had to come along and do it, hanging or no hanging. And I tell you it didnt feel rotten: it felt bully, just bully. Anyhow, I got the rotten feel off me for a minute of my life; and I'll go through fire to get it off me again. Look here! which of you will marry Feemy Evans?

THE BOYS [*uproariously*] Who speaks first? Who'll marry Feemy? Come along, Jack. Nows your chance, Peter. Pass along a husband for Feemy. Oh my! Feemy!

FEEMY [*shortly*] Keep your tongue off me, will you?

BLANCO. Feemy was a rose of the broad path, wasnt she? You all thought her the champion bad woman of this district. Well, she's a failure as a bad woman; and I'm a failure as a bad man. So let Brother Daniels marry us to keep all the rottenness in the family. What do you say, Feemy?

FEEMY. Thank you; but when I marry I'll marry a man that could do a decent action without surprising himself out of his senses. Youre like a child with a new toy: you and your bit of human kindness!

THE WOMAN. How many would have done it with their life at stake?

FEEMY. Oh well, if youre so much taken with him, marry him yourself. Youd be what people call a good wife to him, wouldnt you?

THE WOMAN. I was a good wife to the child's father. I dont think any woman wants to be a good wife twice in her life. I want somebody to be a good husband to me now.

BLANCO. Any offer, gentleman, on that understanding? [*The boys shake their heads*]. Oh, it's a rotten game, our game. Heres a real good woman; and she's had enough of it, finding that it only led to being put upon.

HANNAH. Well, if there was nothing wrong in the world there wouldnt be anything left for us to do, would there?

ELDER DANIELS. Be of good cheer, brothers. Seek the path.

BLANCO. No. No more paths. No more broad and narrow. No more good and bad. There's no good and bad; but by Jiminy, gents, theres a rotten game, and theres a great game. I played the rotten game; but the great game was played on me; and now I'm for the great game every time. Amen. Gentlemen: let us adjourn to the saloon. I stand the drinks. [*He jumps down from the table*].

THE BOYS. Right you are, Blanco. Drinks round. Come along, boys. Blanco's standing. Right along to the Elder's. Hurrah! [*They rush out, dragging the Elder with them*].

BLANCO [*to Feemy, offering his hand*] Shake, Feemy.

FEEMY. Get along, you blackguard.

BLANCO. It's come over me again, same as when the kid touched me, same as when you swore a lie to save my neck.

FEEMY. Oh well, here. [*They shake hands*].

FANNY'S FIRST PLAY:
AN EASY PLAY FOR A LITTLE THEATRE

WITH

Preface

FANNY'S FIRST PLAY

Composition begun 13 August 1910; completed 5 March 1911. First published in German translation, as *Fannis erstes Stück*, in the *Neue Freie Presse* (Vienna), 16 July–8 October 1911. Published in *Misalliance, The Dark Lady of the Sonnets, and Fanny's First Play*, 1914. First presented at the Little Theatre, London, on 19 April 1911, with the authorship concealed.

The Induction

Footman *A. E. Filmer*
Cecil Savoyard *Lewis Sealy*
Count O'Dowda *Harcourt Williams*
Fanny O'Dowda *Christine Silver*
Mr Trotter *Claude King*
Mr Vaughan *S. Creagh Henry*
Gilbert Gunn *Reginald Owen*
Flawner Bannal *Nigel Playfair*

The Play

Robin Gilbey *Fewlass Llewellyn*
Maria Gilbey *Gwynneth Galton*
Juggins the footman *H. K. Ayliff*
Dora Delaney *Dorothy Minto*
Amelia Knox *Cicely Hamilton*
Joseph Knox *Arnold Lucy*
Margaret Knox *Lillah McCarthy*
Lieutenant Duvallet *Raymond Lauzette*
Bobby Gilbey *Shiel Barry*

Period – 1911

The Induction – *The Saloon of Count O'Dowda's Country House in Cambridge. Before the Curtain. Evening*

ACT I *Mr Robin Gilbey's Dining Room, Denmark Hill. Morning*

ACT II *Mr Joseph Knox's Drawing Room in the same Neighborhood. Afternoon*

ACT III *Again in Mr Gilbey's Dining Room. Later the same Afternoon*

Epilogue – *As in the Induction. After the Play*

Fanny's First Play, being but a potboiler, needs no preface. But its lesson is not, I am sorry to say, unneeded. Mere morality, or the substitution of custom for conscience, was once accounted a shameful and cynical thing: people talked of right and wrong, of honor and dishonor, of sin and grace, of salvation and damnation, not of morality and immorality. The word morality, if we met it in the Bible, would surprise us as much as the word telephone or motor car. Nowadays we do not seem to know that there is any other test of conduct except morality; and the result is that the young had better have their souls awakened by disgrace, capture by the police, and a month's hard labor, than drift along from their cradles to their graves doing what other people do for no other reason than that other people do it, and knowing nothing of good and evil, of courage and cowardice, or indeed anything but how to keep hunger and concupiscence and fashionable dressing within the bounds of good taste except when their excesses can be concealed. Is it any wonder that I am driven to offer to young people in our suburbs the desperate advice: Do something that will get you into trouble? But please do not suppose that I defend a state of things which makes such advice the best that can be given under the circumstances, or that I do not know how difficult it is to find out a way of getting into trouble that will combine loss of respectability with integrity of self-respect and reasonable consideration for other people's feelings and interests on every point except their dread of losing their own respectability. But when there's a will there's a way. I hate to see dead people walking about: it is unnatural. And our respectable middle-class people are all as dead as mutton. Out of the mouth of Mrs Knox I have delivered on them the judgment of her God.

The critics whom I have lampooned in the induction to this play under the names of Trotter, Vaughan, and Gunn will forgive me: in fact Mr Trotter forgave me beforehand, and assisted the make-up by which Mr Claude King so successfully simulated his personal appearance. The critics whom I did not introduce were somewhat hurt, as I should have been myself under the same circumstances; but I had not room for them all; so I can only apologize and assure them that I meant no disrespect.

The concealment of the authorship, if a *secret de Polichinelle* can be said to involve concealment, was a necessary part of the play. In so far as it was effectual, it operated as a measure of relief to those critics and playgoers who are so obsessed by my strained legendary reputation that they approach my plays in a condition which is really one of derangement, and are quite unable to conceive a play of mine as anything but a trap baited with paradoxes, and designed to compass their ethical perversion and intellectual confusion. If it were possible, I should put forward all my plays anonymously, or hire some less disturbing person, as Bacon is said to have hired Shakespear, to father my plays for me.

INDUCTION

The end of a saloon in an old-fashioned country-house (Florence Towers, the property of Count O'Dowda) has been curtained off to form a stage for a private theatrical performance. A footman in grandiose Spanish livery enters before the curtain, on its O. P. side.

FOOTMAN [*announcing*] Mr Cecil Savoyard. [*Cecil Savoyard comes in: a middle-aged man in evening dress and a fur-lined overcoat. He is surprised to find nobody to receive him. So is the Footman*]. Oh, beg pardon, sir: I thought the Count was here. He was when I took up your name. He must have gone through the stage into the library. This way, sir. [*He moves towards the division in the middle of the curtains*].

SAVOYARD. Half a mo. [*The Footman stops*]. When does the play begin? Half-past eight?

FOOTMAN. Nine, sir.

SAVOYARD. Oh, good. Well, will you telephone to my wife at the George that it's not until nine?

FOOTMAN. Right, sir. Mrs Cecil Savoyard, sir?

SAVOYARD. No: Mrs William Tinkler. Dont forget.

FOOTMAN. Mrs Tinkler, sir. Right, sir. [*The Count comes in through the curtains*]. Here is the Count, sir. [*Announcing*] Mr Cecil Savoyard, sir. [*He withdraws*].

COUNT O'DOWDA [*a handsome man of fifty, dressed with studied elegance a hundred years out of date, advancing cordially to shake hands with his visitor*] Pray excuse me, Mr Savoyard. I suddenly recollected that all the bookcases in the library were locked – in fact theyve never been opened since we came from Venice – and as our literary guests will probably use the library a good deal, I just ran in to unlock everything.

SAVOYARD. Oh, you mean the dramatic critics. M'yes. I suppose theres a smoking room?

THE COUNT. My study is available. An old-fashioned house, you understand. Wont you sit down, Mr Savoyard?

SAVOYARD. Thanks. [*They sit. Savoyard, looking at his host's obsolete costume, continues*] I had no idea you were going to appear in the piece yourself.

THE COUNT. I am not. I wear this costume because – well, perhaps I had better explain the position, if it interests you.

SAVOYARD. Certainly.

THE COUNT. Well, you see, Mr Savoyard, I'm rather a stranger in your world. I am not, I hope, a modern man in any sense of the word. I'm not really an Englishman: my family is Irish: Ive lived all my life in Italy – in Venice mostly – my very title is a foreign one: I am a Count of the Holy Roman Empire.

SAVOYARD. Where's that?

THE COUNT. At present, nowhere, except as a memory and an ideal. [*Savoyard inclines his head respectfully to the ideal*]. But I am by no means an idealogue. I am not content with beautiful dreams: I want beautiful realities.

SAVOYARD. Hear, hear! I'm all with you there – when you can get them.

THE COUNT. Why not get them? The difficulty is not that there are no beautiful realities, Mr Savoyard: the difficulty is that so few of us know them when we see them. We have inherited from the past a vast treasure of beauty – of imperishable masterpieces of poetry, of painting, of sculpture, of architecture, of music, of exquisite fashions in dress, in furniture, in domestic decoration. We can contemplate these treasures. We can reproduce many of them. We can buy a few inimitable originals. We can shut out the nineteenth century –

SAVOYARD [*correcting him*] The twentieth.

THE COUNT. To me the century I shut out will always be the nineteenth century, just as your national anthem will always be God Save the Queen, no matter how many kings may succeed. I found England befouled with industrialism: well, I did what Byron did: I simply refused to live in it. You remember Byron's words: 'I am sure my bones would not rest in an English grave, or my clay mix with the earth of that country. I believe the thought would drive me mad on my deathbed could I suppose that any of my friends would be base enough to convey my carcase back to her soil. I would not even feed her worms if I could help it.'

SAVOYARD. Did Byron say that?

THE COUNT. He did, sir.

SAVOYARD. It dont sound like him. I saw a good deal of him at one time.

THE COUNT. You! But how is that possible? You are too young.

SAVOYARD. I was quite a lad, of course. But I had a job in the original production of Our Boys.

THE COUNT. My dear sir, not *that* Byron, Lord Byron, the poet.

SAVOYARD. Oh, I beg your pardon. I thought you were talking of *the* Byron. So you prefer living abroad?

THE COUNT. I find England ugly and Philistine. Well, I dont live in it. I find modern houses ugly. I dont live in them: I have a palace on the grand canal. I find modern clothes prosaic. I dont wear them, except, of course, in the street. My ears are offended by the Cockney twang: I keep out of hearing of it and speak and listen to Italian. I find Beethoven's music coarse and restless, and Wagner's senseless and detestable. I do not listen to them: I listen to Cimarosa, to Pergolesi, to Gluck and Mozart. Nothing simpler, sir.

SAVOYARD. It's all right when you can afford it.

THE COUNT. Afford it! My dear Savoyard, if you are a man with a sense of beauty you can make an earthly paradise for yourself in Venice on £1500 a year, whilst our wretched vulgar industrial millionaires are spending twenty thousand on the amusements of billiard markers. I assure you I am a poor man according to modern ideas. But I have never had anything less than the very best that life has produced. It is my good fortune to have a beautiful and lovable daughter; and that girl, sir, has never seen an ugly sight or heard an ugly sound that I could spare her; and she has certainly never worn an ugly dress or tasted coarse food or bad wine in her life. She has lived in a palace; and her perambulator was a gondola. Now you know the sort of people we are, Mr Savoyard. You can imagine how we feel here.

SAVOYARD. Rather out of it, eh?

THE COUNT. Out of it, sir! Out of what?

SAVOYARD. Well, out of everything.

THE COUNT. Out of soot and fog and mud and east wind; out of vulgarity and ugliness, hypocrisy and greed, superstition and stupidity. Out of all this, and in the sunshine, in the enchanted region of which great artists alone have had the secret, in the sacred footsteps of Byron, of Shelley, of the Brownings, of Turner and Ruskin. Dont you envy me, Mr Savoyard?

SAVOYARD. Some of us must live in England, you know, just to keep the place going. Besides – though, mind you, I dont say it isnt all right from the high art point of view and all that – three weeks of it would drive me melancholy mad. However, I'm glad you told me, because it explains why it is you dont seem to know your way about much in England. I hope, by the way, that everything has given satisfaction to your daughter.

THE COUNT. She seems quite satisfied. She tells me that the actors you sent down are perfectly suited to their parts, and very nice people to work with. I understand she had some difficulties at the first rehearsals with the gentleman you call the producer, because he hadnt read the play; but the moment he found out what it was all about everything went smoothly.

SAVOYARD. Havnt you seen the rehearsals?

THE COUNT. Oh no. I havnt been allowed even to meet any of the company. All I can tell you is that the hero is a Frenchman [*Savoyard is rather scandalized*]: I asked her not to have an English hero. That is all I know. [*ruefully*] I havnt been consulted even about the costumes, though there, I think, I could have been some use.

SAVOYARD [*puzzled*] But there arnt any costumes.

THE COUNT [*seriously shocked*] What! No costumes! Do you mean to say it is a modern play?

SAVOYARD. I dont know: I didnt read it. I handed it to Billy Burjoyce – the producer, you know – and left it to him to select the company and so on. But I should have had to order the costumes if there had been any. There wernt.

THE COUNT [*smiling as he recovers from his alarm*] I understand. She has taken the costumes into her own hands. She is an expert in beautiful costumes. I venture to promise you, Mr Savoyard, that what you are about to see will be like a Louis Quatorze ballet painted by Watteau. The heroine will be an exquisite Columbine, her lover a dainty Harlequin, her father a picturesque Pantaloon, and the valet who hoodwinks the father and brings about the happiness of the lovers a grotesque but perfectly tasteful Punchinello or Mascarille or Sganarelle.

SAVOYARD. I see. That makes three men; and the clown and policeman will make five. Thats why you wanted five men in the company.

THE COUNT. My dear sir, you dont suppose I mean that vulgar, ugly, silly, senseless, malicious and destructive thing the harlequinade of a nineteenth century English Christmas pantomime! What was it after all but a stupid attempt to imitate the success made by the genius of Grimaldi a hundred years ago? My daughter does not know of the existence of such a thing. I refer to the graceful and charming fantasies of the Italian and French stages of the seventeenth and eighteenth centuries.

SAVOYARD. Oh, I beg pardon. I quite agree that harlequinades are rot. Theyve been dropped at all smart theatres. But from what Billy Burjoyce told me I got the idea that your daughter knew her way about here, and had seen a lot of plays. He had no idea she'd been away in Venice all the time.

THE COUNT. Oh, she has not been. I should have explained that two years ago my daughter left me to complete her education at Cambridge. Cambridge was my own University; and though of course there were no women there in my time, I felt confident that if the atmosphere of the eighteenth century still existed anywhere in England, it would be at Cambridge. About three months ago she wrote to me and asked whether I wished to give her a present on her next birthday. Of course I said yes; and she then astonished and delighted me by telling me that she had written a play, and that the present she wanted was a private performance of it with real actors and real critics.

SAVOYARD. Yes: thats what staggered me. It was easy enough to engage a company for a private peformance: it's done often enough. But the notion of having critics was new. I hardly knew how to set about it. They dont expect private engagements; and so they have no agents. Besides, I didnt know what to offer them. I knew that they were cheaper than actors, because they get long engagements: forty years sometimes; but thats no rule for a single job. Then theres such a lot of them: on first nights they run away with all your stalls: you cant find a decent place for your own mother. It would have cost a fortune to bring the lot.

THE COUNT. Of course I never dreamt of having them all. Only a few first-rate representative men.

SAVOYARD. Just so. All you want is a few sample opinions. Out of a hundred notices you wont find more than four at the outside that say anything different. Well, Ive got just the right four for you. And what do you think it has cost me?

THE COUNT [*shrugging his shoulders*] I cannot guess.

SAVOYARD. Ten guineas, and expenses. I had to give Flawner Bannal ten. He wouldnt come for less; and he asked fifty. I had to give it, because if we hadnt had him we might just as well have had nobody at all.

THE COUNT. But what about the others, if Mr Flannel –

SAVOYARD [*shocked*] Flawner Bannal.

THE COUNT. – if Mr Bannal got the whole ten?

SAVOYARD. Oh, I managed that. As this is a high-class sort of thing, the first man I went for was Trotter.

THE COUNT. Oh indeed. I am very glad you have secured Mr Trotter. I have read his Playful Impressions.

SAVOYARD. Well, I was rather in a funk about him. He's not exactly what I call approachable; and he was a bit stand-off at first. But when I explained and told him your daughter –

THE COUNT [*interrupting in alarm*] You did not say that the play was by her, I hope?

SAVOYARD. No: thats been kept a dead secret. I just said your daughter has asked for a real play with a real author and a real critic and all the rest of it. The moment I mentioned the daughter I had him. He has a daughter of his own. Wouldnt hear of payment! Offered to come just to please her! Quite human. I was surprised.

THE COUNT. Extremely kind of him.

SAVOYARD. Then I went to Vaughan, because he does music as well as the drama; and you said you thought there would be music. I told him Trotter would feel lonely without him; so he promised like a bird. Then I thought youd like one of the latest sort: the chaps that go for the newest things and swear theyre oldfashioned. So I nailed Gilbert Gunn. The four will give you a representative team. By the way [*looking at his watch*] theyll be here presently.

THE COUNT. Before they come, Mr Savoyard, could you give me any hints about them that would help me to make a little conversation with them? I am, as you said, rather out of it in England; and I might unwittingly say something tactless.

SAVOYARD. Well, let me see. As you dont like English people, I dont know that youll get on with Trotter, because he's thoroughly English: never happy except when he's in Paris, and speaks French so unnecessarily well that everybody there spots him as an Englishman the moment he opens his mouth. Very witty and all that. Pretends to turn up his nose at the theatre and says people make too much fuss about art [*the Count is extremely indignant*]. But thats only his modesty, because art is his own line, you understand. Mind you dont chaff him about Aristotle.

THE COUNT. Why should I chaff him about Aristotle?

SAVOYARD. Well, I dont know; but it's one of the recognized ways of chaffing him. However, youll get on with him all right: he's a man of the world and a man of sense. The one youll have to be careful about is Vaughan.

THE COUNT. In what way, may I ask?

SAVOYARD. Well, Vaughan has no sense of humor; and if you joke with him he'll think youre insulting him on purpose. Mind: it's not that he doesnt see a joke: he does; and it hurts him. A comedy scene makes him sore all over: he goes away black and blue, and pitches into the play for all he's worth.

THE COUNT. But surely that is a very serious defect in a man of his profession?

SAVOYARD. Yes it is, and no mistake. But Vaughan is honest, and dont care a brass farthing what he says, or whether it pleases anybody or not; and you must have one man of that sort to say the things that nobody else will say.

THE COUNT. It seems to me to carry the principle of division of labor too far, this keeping of the honesty and the other qualities in separate compartments. What is Mr Gunn's speciality, if I may ask?

SAVOYARD. Gunn is one of the Intellectuals.

THE COUNT. But arnt they all Intellectuals?

SAVOYARD. Lord! no: heaven forbid! You must be careful what you say about that: I shouldnt like anyone to call me an

Intellectual: I dont think any Englishman would! They dont count really, you know; but still it's rather the thing to have them. Gunn is one of the young Intellectuals: he writes plays himself. He's useful because he pitches into the older Intellectuals who are standing in his way. But you may take it from me that none of these chaps really matter. Flawner Bannal's your man. Bannal really represents the British playgoer. When he likes a thing, you may take your oath there are a hundred thousand people in London thatll like it if they can only be got to know about it. Besides, Bannal's knowledge of the theatre is an inside knowledge. We know him; and he knows us. He knows the ropes: he knows his way about: he knows what he's talking about.

THE COUNT [*with a little sigh*] Age and experience, I suppose?

SAVOYARD. Age! I should put him at twenty at the very outside, myself. It's not an old man's job after all, is it? Bannal may not ride the literary high horse like Trotter and the rest; but I'd take his opinion before any other in London. He's the man in the street; and thats what you want.

THE COUNT. I am almost sorry you didnt give the gentleman his full terms. I should not have grudged the fifty guineas for a sound opinion. He may feel shabbily treated.

SAVOYARD. Well, let him. It was a bit of side, his asking fifty. After all, what is he? Only a pressman. Jolly good business for him to earn ten guineas: he's done the same job often enough for half a quid, I expect.

Fanny O'Dowda comes precipitately through the curtains, excited and nervous. A girl of nineteen in a dress synchronous with her father's.

FANNY. Papa, papa, the critics have come. And one of them has a cocked hat and sword like a – [*she notices Savoyard*] Oh, I beg your pardon.

THE COUNT. This is Mr Savoyard, your impresario, my dear.

FANNY [*shaking hands*] How do you do?

SAVOYARD. Pleased to meet you, Miss O'Dowda. The cocked hat is all right. Trotter is a member of the new Academic Committee. He induced them to go in for a uniform like the French Academy; and I asked him to wear it.

THE FOOTMAN [*announcing*] Mr Trotter, Mr Vaughan, Mr Gunn, Mr Flawner Bannal.

The four critics enter. Trotter wears a diplomatic dress, with sword and three-cornered hat. His age is about 50. Vaughan is 40. Gunn is 30. Flawner Bannal is 20 and is quite unlike the others, who can be classed at sight as professional men whilst Bannal is obviously an unemployable of the business class picking up a living by an obtuse courage which gives him cheerfulness, conviviality, and bounce, and is helped out positively by a slight turn for writing, and negatively by a comfortable ignorance and lack of intuition which hides from him all the dangers and disgraces that keep men of finer perception in check. The Count approaches them hospitably.

SAVOYARD. Count O'Dowda, gentlemen. Mr Trotter.

TROTTER [*looking at the Count's costume*] Have I the pleasure of meeting a *confrère*?

THE COUNT. No, sir: I have no right to my costume except the right of a lover of the arts to dress myself handsomely. You are most welcome, Mr Trotter. [*Trotter bows in the French manner*].

SAVOYARD. Mr Vaughan.

THE COUNT. How do you do, Mr Vaughan?

VAUGHAN. Quite well, thanks.

SAVOYARD. Mr Gunn.

THE COUNT. Delighted to make your acquaintance, Mr Gunn.

GUNN. Very pleased.

SAVOYARD. Mr Flawner Bannal.

THE COUNT. Very kind of you to come, Mr Bannal.

BANNAL. Dont mention it.

THE COUNT. Gentlemen, my daughter. [*They all bow*]. We are very greatly indebted to you, gentlemen, for so kindly indulging her whim. [*The dressing bell sounds. The Count looks at his watch*]. Ah! The dressing bell, gentlemen. As our play begins at nine, I have had to put forward the dinner hour a little. May I shew you to your rooms? [*He goes out, followed by all the men, except Trotter, who, going last, is detained by Fanny*].

FANNY. Mr Trotter: I want to say something to you about this play.

TROTTER. No: thats forbidden. You must not attempt to *souffler* the critic.

FANNY. Oh, I would not for the world try to influence your opinion.

TROTTER. But you do: you are influencing me very shockingly. You invite me to this charming house, where I'm about to enjoy a charming dinner. And just before the dinner I'm taken aside by a charming young lady to be talked to about the play. How can you expect me to be impartial? God forbid that I should set up to be a judge, or do more than record an impression; but my impressions can be influenced; and in this case youre influencing them shamelessly all the time.

FANNY. Dont make me more nervous than I am already, Mr Trotter. If you knew how I feel!

TROTTER. Naturally: your first party: your first appearance in England as hostess. But youre doing it beautifully. Dont be afraid. Every *nuance* is perfect.

FANNY. It's so kind of you to say so, Mr Trotter. But that isnt whats the matter. The truth is, this play is going to give my father a dreadful shock.

TROTTER. Nothing unusual in that, I'm sorry to say. Half the young ladies in London spend their evenings making their fathers take them to plays that are not fit for elderly people to see.

FANNY. Oh, I know all about that; but you cant understand what it means to papa. Youre not so innocent as he is.

TROTTER [*remonstrating*] My dear young lady –

FANNY. I dont mean morally innocent: everybody who reads your articles knows youre as innocent as a lamb.

TROTTER. What!

FANNY. Yes, Mr Trotter: Ive seen a good deal of life since I came to England; and I assure you that to me youre a mere baby: a dear, good, well-meaning, delightful, witty, charming baby; but still just a wee lamb in a world of wolves. Cambridge is not what it was in my father's time.

TROTTER. Well, I must say!

FANNY. Just so. Thats one of our classifications in the Cambridge Fabian Society.

TROTTER. Classifications? I dont understand.

FANNY. We classify our aunts into different sorts. And one of the sorts is the 'I must says'.

TROTTER. I withdraw 'I must say'. I substitute 'Blame my cats!' No: I substitute 'Blame my kittens!' Observe, Miss O'Dowda: kittens. I say again in the teeth of the whole Cambridge Fabian Society, kittens. Impertinent little kittens. Blame them. Smack them. I guess what is on your conscience. This play to which you have lured me is one of those in which members of Fabian Societies instruct their grandmothers in the art of milking ducks. And you are afraid it will shock your father. Well, I hope it will. And if he consults me about it I shall recommend him to smack you soundly and pack you off to bed.

FANNY. Thats one of your prettiest literary attitudes, Mr Trotter, but it doesnt take me in. You see, I'm much more conscious of what you really are than you are yourself, because weve discussed you thoroughly at Cambridge; and youve never discussed yourself, have you?

TROTTER. I –

FANNY. Of course you havnt; so you see it's no good Trottering at me.

TROTTER. Trottering!

FANNY. Thats what we call it at Cambridge.

TROTTER. If it were not so obviously a stage *cliché*, I should say Damn Cambridge. As it is, I blame my kittens. And now let me warn you. If youre going to be a charming healthy young English girl, you may coax me. If youre going to be an unsexed Cambridge Fabian virago, I'll treat you as my intellectual equal, as I would treat a man.

FANNY [*adoringly*] But how few men are your intellectual equals, Mr Trotter!

TROTTER. I'm getting the worst of this.

FANNY. Oh no. Why do you say that?

TROTTER. May I remind you that the dinner-bell will ring presently?

FANNY. What does it matter! We're both ready. I havnt told you yet what I want you to do for me.

TROTTER. Nor have you particularly predisposed me to do it, except out of pure magnanimity. What is it?

FANNY. I dont mind this play shocking my father morally. It's good for him to be shocked morally. It's all that the young can do for the old, to shock them and keep them up to date. But I know that this play will shock him artistically; and that terrifies me. No moral consideration could make a breach between us: he would forgive me for anything of that kind sooner or later; but he never gives way on a point of art. I darent let him know that I love Beethoven and Wagner; and as to Strauss, if he heard three bars of Elektra, it'd part us for ever. Now what I want you to do is this. If he's very angry – if he hates the play, because it's a modern play – will you tell him that it's not my fault; that its style and construction, and so forth, are considered the very highest art nowadays; that the author wrote it in the proper way for repertory theatres of the most superior kind – you know the kind of plays I mean?

TROTTER [*emphatically*] I think I know the sort of entertainments you mean. But please do not beg a vital question by calling them plays. I dont pretend to be an authority; but I have at least established the fact that these productions, whatever else they may be, are certainly not plays.

FANNY. The authors dont say they are.

TROTTER [*emphatically*] I think I know the sort of entertainments say, a personal friend of mine, resorts freely to the dastardly subterfuge of calling them conversations, discussions, and so forth, with the express object of evading criticism. But I'm not to be disarmed by such tricks. I say they are not plays. Dialogues, if you will. Exhibitions of character, perhaps: especially the character of the author. Fiction, possibly, though a little decent reticence as to introducing actual persons, and thus violating the sanctity of private life, might not be amiss. But plays, no. I say NO. Not plays. If you will not concede this point I cant continue our conversation. I take this seriously. It's a matter of principle. I must ask you. Miss O'Dowda, before we go a step further, Do you or do you not claim that these works are plays?

FANNY. I assure you I dont.

TROTTER. Not in any sense of the word?

FANNY. Not in any sense of the word. I loathe plays.

TROTTER [*disappointed*] That last remark destroys all the value of your admission. You admire these – these theatrical nondescripts? You enjoy them?

FANNY. Dont you?

TROTTER. Of course I do. Do you take me for a fool? Do you suppose I prefer popular melodramas? Have I not written most appreciative notices of them? But I say theyre not plays. Theyre not plays. I cant consent to remain in this house another minute if anything remotely resembling them is to be foisted on me as a play.

FANNY. I fully admit that theyre not plays. I only want you to tell my father that plays are not plays nowadays – not in your sense of the word.

TROTTER. Ah, there you go again! In my sense of the word! You believe that my criticism is merely a personal impression; that –

FANNY. You always said it was.

TROTTER. Pardon me: not on this point. If you had been classically educated –

FANNY. But I have.

TROTTER. Pooh! Cambridge! If you had been educated at Oxford, you would know that the definition of a play has been settled exactly and scientifically for two thousand two hundred and sixty years. When I say that these entertainments are not plays, I dont mean in my sense of the word, but in the sense given to it for all time by the immortal Stagirite.

FANNY. Who is the Stagirite?

TROTTER [*shocked*] You dont know who the Stagirite was!

FANNY. Sorry. Never heard of him.

TROTTER. And this is Cambridge education! Well, my dear young lady, I'm delighted to find theres something you dont know; and I shant spoil you by dispelling an ignorance which, in my opinion, is highly becoming to your age and sex. So we'll leave it at that.

FANNY. But you will promise to tell my father that lots of people write plays just like this one – that I havnt selected it out of mere heartlessness?

TROTTER. I cant possibly tell you what I shall say to your father about the play until Ive seen the play. But I'll tell you what I shall say to him about you. I shall say that youre a very foolish young lady; that youve got into a very questionable set; and that the sooner he takes you away from Cambridge and its Fabian Society, the better.

FANNY. It's so funny to hear you pretending to be a heavy father. In Cambridge we regard you as a *bel esprit*, a wit, an Irresponsible, a Parisian Immoralist, *très chic*.

TROTTER. I!

FANNY. Theres quite a Trotter set.

TROTTER. Well, upon my word!

FANNY. They go in for adventures and call you Aramis.

TROTTER. They wouldnt dare!

FANNY. You always make such delicious fun of the serious people. Your *insouciance* –

TROTTER [*frantic*] Stop talking French to me: it's not a proper language for a young girl. Great heavens! how is it possible that a few innocent pleasantries should be so frightfully misunderstood? Ive tried all my life to be sincere and simple, to be unassuming and kindly. Ive lived a blameless life. Ive supported the Censorship in the face of ridicule and insult. And now I'm told that I'm a centre of Immoralism! of Modern Minxism! a trifler with the most sacred subjects! a Nietzschean!! perhaps a Shavian!!!

FANNY. Do you mean you are really on the serious side, Mr Trotter?

TROTTER. Of course I'm on the serious side. How dare you ask me such a question?

FANNY. Then why dont you play for it?

TROTTER. I do play for it – short, of course, of making myself ridiculous.

FANNY. What! not make yourself ridiculous for the sake of a good cause! Oh, Mr Trotter! Thats *vieux jeu*.

TROTTER [*shouting at her*] Dont talk French. I will not allow it.

FANNY. But this dread of ridicule is so frightfully out of date. The Cambridge Fabian Society –

TROTTER. I forbid you to mention the Fabian Society to me.

FANNY. Its motto is 'You cannot learn to skate without making yourself ridiculous.'

TROTTER. Skate! What has that to do with it?

FANNY. Thats not all. It goes on, 'The ice of life is slippery.'

TROTTER. Ice of life indeed! You should be eating penny ices and enjoying yourself. I wont hear another word.

The Count returns.

THE COUNT. We're all waiting in the drawing room, my dear. Have you been detaining Mr Trotter all this time?

TROTTER. I'm so sorry. I must have just a little brush up: I – [*He hurries out*].

THE COUNT. My dear, you should be in the drawing room. You should not have kept him here.

FANNY. I know. Dont scold me: I had something important to say to him.

THE COUNT. I shall ask him to take you in to dinner.

FANNY. Yes, papa. Oh, I hope it will go off well.

THE COUNT. Yes, love, of course it will. Come along.

FANNY. Just one thing, papa, while we're alone. Who was the Stagirite?

THE COUNT. The Stagirite! Do you mean to say you dont know?

FANNY. Havnt the least notion.

THE COUNT. The Stagirite was Aristotle. By the way, dont mention him to Mr Trotter.

They go to the dining room.

ACT I

In the dining room of a house in Denmark Hill, an elderly lady sits at breakfast reading the newspaper. Her chair is at the end of the oblong dining table furthest from the fire. There is an empty chair at the other end. The fireplace is behind this chair; and the door is next the fireplace, between it and the corner. An armchair stands beside the coal-scuttle. In the middle of the back wall is the sideboard, parallel to the table. The rest of the furniture is mostly dining-room chairs, ranged against the walls, and including a baby rocking chair on the lady's side of the room. The lady is a placid person. Her husband, Mr Robin Gilbey, not at all placid, bursts violently into the room with a letter in his hand.

GILBEY [*grinding his teeth*] This is a nice thing. This is a b –

MRS GILBEY [*cutting him short*] Leave it at that, please. Whatever it is, bad language wont make it better.

GILBEY [*bitterly*] Yes, put me in the wrong as usual. Take your boy's part against me. [*He flings himself into the empty chair opposite her*].

MRS GILBEY. When he does anything right, he's your son. When he does anything wrong he's mine. Have you any news of him?

GILBEY. Ive a good mind not to tell you.

MRS GILBEY. Then dont. I suppose he's been found. Thats a comfort, at all events.

GILBEY. No, he hasnt been found. The boy may be at the bottom of the river for all you care. [*Too agitated to sit quietly, he rises and paces the room distractedly*].

MRS GILBEY. Then what have you got in your hand?

GILBEY. Ive a letter from the Monsignor Grenfell. From New York. Dropping us. Cutting us. [*turning fiercely on her*] Thats a nice thing, isnt it?

MRS GILBEY. What for?

GILBEY [*flinging away towards his chair*] How do *I* know what for?

MRS GILBEY. What does he say?

GILBEY [*sitting down and grumblingly adjusting his spectacles*] This is what he says. 'My dear Mr Gilbey: The news about Bobby had to follow me across the Atlantic: it did not reach me until to-day. I am afraid he is incorrigible. My brother, as you may imagine, feels that this last escapade has gone beyond the bounds; and I think, myself, that Bobby ought to be made to feel that such scrapes involve a certain degree of reprobation.' 'As you may imagine!' And we know no more about it than the babe unborn.

MRS GILBEY. What else does he say?

GILBEY. 'I think my brother must have been just a little to blame himself; so, between ourselves, I shall, with due and impressive formality, forgive Bobby later on; but for the present I think it had better be understood that he is in disgrace, and that we are no longer on visiting terms. As ever, yours sincerely.' [*His agitation masters him again*] Thats a nice slap in the face to get from a man in his position! This is what your son has brought on me.

MRS GILBEY. Well, I think it's rather a nice letter. He as good as tells you he's only letting on to be offended for Bobby's good.

GILBEY. Oh, very well: have the letter framed and hang it up over the mantelpiece as a testimonial.

MRS GILBEY. Dont talk nonsense, Rob. You ought to be thankful to know that the boy is alive after his disappearing like that for nearly a week.

GILBEY. Nearly a week! A fortnight, you mean. Wheres your feelings, woman! It was fourteen days yesterday.

MRS GILBEY. Oh, dont call it fourteen days, Rob, as if the boy was in prison.

GILBEY. How do you know he's not in prison? It's got on my nerves so, that I'd believe even that.

MRS GILBEY. Dont talk silly, Rob. Bobby might get into a scrape like any other lad; but he'd never do anything low.

Juggins, the footman, comes in with a card on a salver. He is a rather low-spirited man of thirty-five or more, of good appearance and address, and iron self-command.

JUGGINS [*presenting the salver to Mr Gilbey*] Lady wishes to see Mr Bobby's parents, sir.

GILBEY [*pointing to Mrs Gilbey*] Theres Mr Bobby's parent. I disown him.

JUGGINS. Yes, sir. [*He presents the salver to Mrs Gilbey*].

MRS GILBEY. You mustnt mind what your master says, Juggins: he doesnt mean it. [*She takes the card and reads it*]. Well, I never!

GILBEY. Whats up now?

MRS GILBEY [*reading*] 'Miss D. Delaney. Darling Dora.' Just like that – in brackets. What sort of person, Juggins?

GILBEY. Whats her address?

MRS GILBEY. The West Circular Road. Is that a respectable address, Juggins?

JUGGINS. A great many most respectable people live in the West Circular Road, madam; but the address is not a guarantee of respectability.

GILBEY. So it's come to that with him, has it?

MRS GILBEY. Dont jump to conclusions, Rob. How do you know? [*To Juggins*] Is she a lady, Juggins? You know what I mean.

JUGGINS. In the sense in which you are using the word, no, madam.

MRS GILBEY. I'd better try what I can get out of her. [*To Juggins*] Shew her up. You dont mind, do you, Rob?

GILBEY. So long as you dont flounce out and leave me alone with her. [*He rises and plants himself on the hearth-rug*].

Juggins goes out.

MRS GILBEY. I wonder what she wants, Rob?

GILBEY. If she wants money, she shant have it. Not a farthing. A nice thing, everybody seeing her on our doorstep! If it wasnt that she may tell us something about the lad, I'd have Juggins put the hussy into the street.

JUGGINS [*returning and announcing*] Miss Delaney. [*He waits for express orders before placing a chair for this visitor*].

Miss Delaney comes in. She is a young lady of hilarious disposition, very tolerable good looks, and killing clothes. She is so affable and confidential that it is very difficult to keep her at a distance by any process short of flinging her out of the house.

DORA [*plunging at once into privileged intimacy and into the middle of the room*] How d'ye do, both. I'm a friend of Bobby's. He told me all about you once, in a moment of confidence. Of course he never let on who he was at the police court.

GILBEY. Police court?

MRS GILBEY [*looking apprehensively at Juggins*] Tch –! Juggins: a chair.

DORA. Oh, Ive let it out, have I! [*Contemplating Juggins approvingly as he places a chair for her between the table and the sideboard*] But he's the right sort: I can see that. [*Buttonholing him*] You wont let on downstairs, old man, will you?

JUGGINS. The family can rely on my absolute discretion. [*He withdraws*].

DORA [*sitting down genteelly*] I dont know what youll say to me: you know I really have no right to come here; but then what was I to do? You know Holy Joe, Bobby's tutor, dont you? But of course you do.

GILBEY [*with dignity*] I know Mr Joseph Grenfell, the brother of Monsignor Grenfell, if it is of him you are speaking.

DORA [*wide-eyed and much amused*] No!!! You dont tell me that old geezer has a brother a Monsignor! And youre Catholics! And I never knew it, though Ive known Bobby ever so long! But of course the last thing you find out about a person is their religion, isnt it?

MRS GILBEY. We're not Catholics. But when the Samuelses got an Archdeacon's son to form their boy's mind, Mr Gilbey thought Bobby ought to have a chance too. And the Monsignor is a customer. Mr Gilbey consulted him about Bobby; and he recommended a brother of his that was more sinned against than sinning.

GILBEY [*on tenterhooks*] She dont want to hear about that, Maria. [*To Dora*] Whats your business?

DORA. I'm afraid it was all my fault.

GILBEY. What was all your fault? I'm half distracted. I dont know what has happened to the boy: he's been lost these fourteen days –

MRS GILBEY. A fortnight, Rob.

GILBEY. – and not a word have we heard of him since.

MRS GILBEY. Dont fuss, Rob.

GILBEY [*yelling*] I will fuss. Youve no feeling. You dont care what becomes of the lad [*He sits down savagely*].

DORA [*soothingly*] Youve been anxious about him. Of course. How thoughtless of me not to begin by telling you he's quite safe. Indeed he's in the safest place in the world, as one may say: safe under lock and key.

GILBEY [*horrified, pitiable*] Oh my – [*his breath fails him*]. Do you mean that when he was in the police court he was in the dock?

Oh, Maria! Oh, great Lord! What has he done? What has he got for it? [*Desperate*] Will you tell me or will you see me go mad on my own carpet?

DORA [*sweetly*] Yes, old dear –

MRS GILBEY [*starting at the familiarity*] Well!

DORA [*continuing*] I'll tell you; but dont you worry: he's all right. I came out myself this morning: there was such a crowd! and a band! they thought I was a suffraget: only fancy! You see it was like this. Holy Joe got talking about how he'd been a champion sprinter at college.

MRS GILBEY. A what?

DORA. A sprinter. He said he was the fastest hundred yards runner in England. We were all in the old cowshed that night.

MRS GILBEY. What old cowshed?

GILBEY [*groaning*] Oh, get on. Get on.

DORA. Oh, of course, you wouldnt know. How silly of me! It's a rather go-ahead sort of music hall in Stepney. We call it the old cowshed.

MRS GILBEY. Does Mr Grenfell take Bobby to music halls?

DORA. No: Bobby takes him. But Holy Joe likes it: fairly laps it up like a kitten, poor old dear. Well, Bobby says to me, 'Darling –'

MRS GILBEY [*placidly*] Why does he call you darling?

DORA. Oh, everybody calls me darling: it's a sort of name Ive got. Darling Dora, you know. Well, he says, 'Darling, if you can get Holy Joe to sprint a hundred yards, I'll stand you that squiffer with the gold keys.'

MRS GILBEY. Does he call his tutor Holy Joe to his face?

Gilbey clutches at his hair in his impatience.

DORA. Well, what would he call him? After all, Holy Joe is Holy Joe; and boys will be boys.

MRS GILBEY. Whats a squiffer?

DORA. Oh, of course: excuse my vulgarity: a concertina. Theres one in a shop in Green Street, ivory inlaid, with gold keys and Russia leather bellows; and Bobby knew I hankered after it; but he couldnt afford it, poor lad, though I knew he just longed to give it to me.

GILBEY. Maria: if you keep interrupting with silly questions, I shall go out of my senses. Heres the boy in gaol and me disgraced for ever; and all you care to know is what a squiffer is.

DORA. Well, remember it has gold keys. The man wouldnt take a penny less than £15 for it. It was a presentation one.

GILBEY [*shouting at her*] Wheres my son? Whats happened to my son? Will you tell me that, and stop cackling about your squiffer?

DORA. Oh, aint we impatient! Well, it does you credit, old dear. And you neednt fuss: theres no disgrace. Bobby behaved like a perfect gentleman. Besides, it was all my fault, I'll own it: I took too much champagne. I was not what you might call drunk; but I was bright, and a little beyond myself; and – I'll confess it – I wanted to shew off before Bobby, because he was a bit taken by a woman on the stage; and she was pretending to be game for anything. You see youve brought Bobby up too strict; and when he gets loose theres no holding him. He does enjoy life more than any lad I ever met.

GILBEY. Never you mind how he's been brought up: thats my business. Tell me how he's been brought down: thats yours.

MRS GILBEY. Oh, dont be rude to the lady, Rob.

DORA. I'm coming to it, old dear: dont you be so headstrong. Well, it was a beautiful moonlight night; and we couldnt get a cab on the nod; so we started to walk, very jolly, you know: arm in arm, and dancing along, singing and all that. When we came into Jamaica Square, there was a young copper on point duty at the corner. I says to Bob: 'Dearie boy: is it a bargain about the squiffer if I make Joe sprint for you?' 'Anything you like, darling,' says he: 'I love you.' I put on my best company manners and stepped up to the copper. 'If you please, sir,' says I, 'can you direct me to Carrickmines Square?' I was so genteel, and talked so sweet, that he fell to it like a bird. 'I never heard of any such Square in these parts,' he says. 'Then,' says I, 'what a very silly little officer you must be!'; and I gave his helmet a chuck behind that knocked it over his eyes, and did a bunk.

MRS GILBEY. Did a what?

DORA. A bunk. Holy Joe did one too all right: he sprinted faster than he ever did in college, I bet, the old dear. He got clean off, too. Just as he was overtaking me half-way down the square, we heard the whistle; and at the sound of it he drew away like a streak of lightning; and that was the last I saw of him. I was copped in the Dock Road myself: rotten luck, wasnt it? I tried the innocent and genteel and all the rest; but Bobby's hat done me in.

GILBEY. And what happened to the boy?

DORA. Only fancy! he stopped to laugh at the copper! He thought the copper would see the joke, poor lamb. He was arguing about it when the two that took me came along to find out what the whistle was for, and brought me with them. Of course I swore I'd never seen him before in my life; but there he was in my hat and I in his. The cops were very spiteful and laid it on for all they were worth: drunk and disorderly and assaulting the police and all that. I got fourteen days without the option, because you see – well, the fact is, I'd done it before, and been warned. Bobby was a first offender and had the option; but the dear boy had no money left and wouldnt give you away by telling his name; and anyhow he couldnt have brought himself to buy himself off and leave me there; so he's doing his month. Well, it was two forty shillingses; and Ive only twenty-eight shillings in the world. If I pawn my clothes I shant be able to earn any more. So I cant pay the fine and get him out; but if youll stand £3 I'll stand one; and thatll do it. If youd like to be very kind and nice you could pay the lot; but I cant deny that it was my fault; so I wont press you.

GILBEY [*heart-broken*] My son in gaol!

DORA. Oh, cheer up, old dear: it wont hurt him: look at me after fourteen days of it: I'm all the better for being kept a bit quiet. You mustnt let it prey on your mind.

GILBEY. The disgrace of it will kill me. And it will leave a mark on him to the end of his life.

DORA. Not a bit of it. Dont you be afraid: Ive educated Bobby a bit: he's not the mollycoddle he was when you had him in hand.

MRS GILBEY. Indeed Bobby is not a mollycoddle. They wanted him to go in for singlestick at the Young Men's Christian Association; but, of course, I couldnt allow that: he might have had his eye knocked out.

GILBEY [*to Dora, angrily*] Listen here, you.

DORA. Oh, aint we cross!

GILBEY. I want none of your gaiety here. This is a respectable household. Youve gone and got my poor innocent boy into trouble. It's the like of you thats the ruin of the like of him.

DORA. So you always say, you old dears. But you know better. Bobby came to me: I didnt come to him.

GILBEY. Would he have gone if you hadnt been there for him to go to? Tell me that. You know why he went to you, I suppose.

DORA [*charitably*] It was dull for him at home, poor lad, wasnt it?

MRS GILBEY. Oh no. I'm at home on first Thursdays. And we have the Knoxes to dinner every Friday. Margaret Knox and Bobby are as good as engaged. Mr Knox is my husband's partner. Mrs Knox is very religious; but she's quite cheerful. We dine with them on Tuesdays. So thats two evenings pleasure every week.

GILBEY [*almost in tears*] We done what we could for the boy. Short of letting him go into temptations of all sorts, he can do what he likes. What more does he want?

DORA. Well, old dear, he wants me and thats about the long and short of it. And I must say youre not very nice to me about it. Ive talked to him like a mother, and tried my best to keep him straight; but I dont deny I like a bit of fun myself; and we both get a bit giddy when we're lighthearted. Him and me is a pair, I'm afraid.

GILBEY. Dont talk foolishness, girl. How could you and he be a pair, you being what you are, and he brought up as he has been, with the example of a religious woman like Mrs Knox before his eyes? I cant understand how he could bring himself to be seen in the street with you. [*Pitying himself*] I havnt deserved this. Ive done my duty as a father. Ive kept him sheltered. [*Angry with her*] Creatures like you that take advantage of a child's innocence ought to be whipped through the streets.

DORA. Well, whatever I may be, I'm too much the lady to lose my temper; and I dont think Bobby would like me to tell you what I think of you; for when I start giving people a bit of my mind I sometimes use language thats beneath me. But I tell you once for all I must have the money to get Bobby out; and if you wont fork out, I'll hunt up Holy Joe. He might get it off his brother, the Monsignor.

GILBEY. You mind your own concerns. My solicitor will do what is right. I'll not have you paying my son's fine as if you were anything to him.

DORA. Thats right. Youll get him out today, wont you?

GILBEY. It's likely I'd leave my boy in prison, isnt it?

DORA. I'd like to know when theyll let him out.

GILBEY. You would, would you? Youre going to meet him at the prison door.

DORA. Well, dont you think any woman would that had the feelings of a lady?

GILBEY [*bitterly*] Oh yes: I know. Here! I must buy the lad's salvation, I suppose. How much will you take to clear out and let him go?

DORA [*pitying him: quite nice about it*] What good would that do, old dear? There are others, you know.

GILBEY. Thats true. I must send the boy himself away.

DORA. Where to?

GILBEY. Anywhere, so long as he's out of the reach of you and your like.

DORA. Then I'm afraid youll have to send him out of the world, old dear. I'm sorry for you: I really am, though you mightnt believe it; and I think your feelings do you real credit. But I cant give him up just to let him fall into the hands of people I couldnt trust, can I?

GILBEY [*beside himself, rising*] Wheres the police? Wheres the Government? Wheres the Church? Wheres respectability and right reason? Whats the good of them if I have to stand here and see you put my son in your pocket as if he was a chattel slave, and you hardly out of gaol as a common drunk and disorderly? Whats the world coming to?

DORA. It is a lottery, isnt it, old dear?

My Gilbey rushes from the room, distracted.

MRS GILBEY [*unruffled*] Where did you buy that white lace? I want some to match a collaret of my own; and I cant get it at Perry and John's.

DORA. Knagg and Pantle's: one and fourpence. It's machine hand-made.

MRS GILBEY. I never give more than one and tuppence. But I

suppose youre extravagant by nature. My sister Martha was just like that. Pay anything she was asked.

DORA. Whats tuppence to you, Mrs Bobby, after all?

MRS GILBEY [*correcting her*] Mrs Gilbey.

DORA. Of course, Mrs Gilbey. I am silly.

MRS GILBEY. Bobby must have looked funny in your hat. Why did you change hats with him?

DORA. I dont know. One does, you know.

MRS GILBEY. I never did. The things people do! I cant understand them. Bobby never told me he was keeping company with you. His own mother!

DORA [*overcome*] Excuse me: I cant help smiling.

Juggins enters.

JUGGINS. Mr Gilbey has gone to Wormwood Scrubs, madam.

MRS GILBEY. Have you ever been in a police court, Juggins?

JUGGINS. Yes, madam.

MRS GILBEY [*rather shocked*] I hope you had not been exceeding, Juggins.

JUGGINS. Yes, madam, I had. I exceeded the legal limit.

MRS GILBEY. Oh, that! Why do they give a woman a fortnight for wearing a man's hat, and a man a month for wearing hers?

JUGGINS. I didnt know that they did, madam.

MRS GILBEY. It doesnt seem justice, does it, Juggins?

JUGGINS. No, madam.

MRS GILBEY [*to Dora, rising*] Well, goodbye. [*Shaking her hand*] So pleased to have made your acquaintance.

DORA [*standing up*] Dont mention it. I'm sure it's most kind of you to receive me at all.

MRS GILBEY. I must go off now and order lunch. [*She trots to the door*]. What was it you called the concertina?

DORA. A squiffer, dear.

MRS GILBEY [*thoughtfully*] A squiffer, of course. How funny! [*She goes out*].

DORA [*exploding into ecstasies of mirth*] Oh my! isnt she an old love? How do you keep your face straight?

JUGGINS. It is what I am paid for.

DORA [*confidentially*] Listen here, dear boy. Your name isnt Juggins. Nobody's name is Juggins.

JUGGINS. My orders are, Miss Delaney, that you are not to be here when Mr Gilbey returns from Wormwood Scrubs.

DORA. That means telling me to mind my own business, doesnt it? Well, I'm off. Tootle Loo, Charlie Darling. [*She kisses her hand to him and goes*].

ACT II

On the afternoon of the same day, Mrs Knox is writing notes in her drawing room, at a writing-table which stands against the wall. Anyone placed so as to see Mrs Knox's left profile, will have the door on the right and the window on the left, both further away than Mrs Knox, whose back is presented to an obsolete upright piano at the opposite side of the room. The sofa is near the piano. There is a small table in the middle of the room, with some gilt-edged books and albums on it, and chairs near it.

Mr Knox comes in almost furtively, a troubled man of fifty, thinner, harder, and uglier than his partner, Gilbey, Gilbey being a soft stoutish man with white hair and thin smooth skin, whilst Knox has coarse black hair, and blue jaws which no diligence in shaving can whiten. Mrs Knox is a plain woman, dressed without regard to fashion, with thoughtful eyes and thoughtful ways that make an atmosphere of peace and some solemnity. She is surprised to see her husband at home during business hours.

MRS KNOX. What brings you home at this hour? Have you heard anything?

KNOX. No. Have you?

MRS KNOX. No. Whats the matter?

KNOX [*sitting down on the sofa*] I believe Gilbey has found out.

MRS KNOX. What makes you think that?

KNOX. Well, I dont know: I didnt like to tell you: you have enough to worry you without that; but Gilbey's been very queer ever since it happened. I cant keep my mind on business as I ought; and I was depending on him. But he's worse than me. He's not looking after anything; and he keeps out of my way. His manner's not natural. He hasnt asked us to dinner; and he's never said a word about our not asking him to dinner, after all these years when weve dined every week as regular as clock-work. It looks to me as if Gilbey's trying to drop me socially. Well, why should he do that if he hasnt heard?

MRS KNOX. I wonder! Bobby hasnt been near us either: thats what I cant make out.

KNOX. Oh, thats nothing. I told him Margaret was down in Cornwall with her aunt.

MRS KNOX [*reproachfully*] Jo! [*She takes her handkerchief from the writing-table and cries a little*].

KNOX. Well, I got to tell lies, aint I? You wont. Somebody's got to tell em.

MRS KNOX [*putting away her handkerchief*] It only ends in our not knowing what to believe. Mrs Gilbey told me Bobby was in Brighton for the sea air. Theres something queer about that. Gilbey would never let the boy loose by himself among the temptations of a gay place like Brighton without his tutor; and I saw the tutor in Kensington High Street the very day she told me.

KNOX. If the Gilbeys have found out, it's all over between Bobby and Margaret, and all over between us and them.

MRS KNOX. It's all over between us and everybody. When a girl runs away from home like that, people know what to think of her and her parents.

KNOX. She had a happy, respectable home – everything –

MRS KNOX [*interrupting him*] Theres no use going over it all again, Jo. If a girl hasnt happiness in herself, she wont be happy anywhere. Youd better go back to the shop and try to keep your mind off it.

KNOX [*rising restlessly*] I cant. I keep fancying everybody knows it and is sniggering about it. I'm at peace nowhere but here. It's a comfort to be with you. It's a torment to be with other people.

MRS KNOX [*going to him and drawing her arm through his*] There, Jo, there! I'm sure I'd have you here always if I could. But it cant be. God's work must go on from day to day, no matter what comes. We must face our trouble and bear it.

KNOX [*wandering to the window arm in arm with her*] Just look at the people in the street, going up and down as if nothing had happened. It seems unnatural, as if they all knew and didnt care.

MRS KNOX. If they knew, Jo, there'd be a crowd round the house looking up at us. You shouldnt keep thinking about it.

KNOX. I know I shouldnt. You have your religion, Amelia; and I'm sure I'm glad it comforts you. But it doesnt come to me that way. Ive worked hard to get a position and be respectable. Ive turned many a girl out of the shop for being half an hour late at night; and heres my own daughter gone for a fortnight without word or sign, except a telegram to say she's not dead and that we're not to worry about her.

MRS KNOX [*suddenly pointing to the street*] Jo, look!

KNOX. Margaret! With a man!

MRS KNOX. Run down, Jo, quick. Catch her: save her.

KNOX [*lingering*] She's shaking hands with him: she's coming across to the door.

MRS KNOX [*energetically*] Do as I tell you. Catch the man before he's out of sight.

Knox rushes from the room. Mrs Knox looks anxiously and excitedly from the window. Then she throws up the sash and leans out. Margaret Knox comes in, flustered and annoyed. She is a strong, springy girl of eighteen, with large nostrils, an audacious chin, and a gaily resolute manner, even peremptory on occasions like the present, when she is annoyed.

MARGARET. Mother. Mother.

Mrs Knox draws in her head and confronts her daughter.

MRS KNOX [*sternly*] Well, miss?

MARGARET. Oh, mother, do go out and stop father making a scene in the street. He rushed at him and said 'Youre the man who took away my daughter' loud enough for all the people to hear. Everybody stopped. We shall have a crowd round the house. Do do something to stop him.

Knox returns with a good-looking young marine officer.

MARGARET. Oh, Monsieur Duvallet, I'm so sorry – so ashamed. Mother: this is Monsieur Duvallet, who has been extremely kind to me. Monsieur Duvallet: my mother. [*Duvallet bows*].

KNOX. A Frenchman! It only needed this.

MARGARET [*much annoyed*] Father: do please be commonly civil to a gentleman who has been of the greatest service to me. What will he think of us?

DUVALLET [*debonair*] But it's very natural. I understand Mr Knox's feelings perfectly. [*He speaks English better than Knox, having learnt it on both sides of the Atlantic*].

KNOX. If Ive made any mistake I'm ready to apologize. But I want to know where my daughter has been for the last fortnight.

DUVALLET. She has been, I assure you, in a particularly safe place.

KNOX. Will you tell me what place? I can judge for myself how safe it was.

MARGARET. Holloway Gaol. Was that safe enough?

KNOX AND MRS KNOX. Holloway Gaol!

KNOX. Youve joined the Suffragets!

MARGARET. No. I wish I had. I could have had the same experience in better company. Please sit down, Monsieur Duvallet. [*She sits between the table and the sofa. Mrs Knox, overwhelmed, sits at the other side of the table. Knox remains standing in the middle of the room*].

DUVALLET [*sitting down on the sofa*] It was nothing. An adventure. Nothing.

MARGARET [*obdurately*] Drunk and assaulting the police! Forty shillings or a month!

MRS KNOX. Margaret! Who accused you of such a thing?

MARGARET. The policeman I assaulted.

KNOX. You mean to say that you did it!

MARGARET. I did. I had that satisfaction at all events. I knocked two of his teeth out.

KNOX. And you sit there coolly and tell me this!

MARGARET. Well, where do you want me to sit? Whats the use of saying things like that?

KNOX. My daughter in Holloway Gaol!

MARGARET. All the women in Holloway are somebody's daughters. Really, father, you must make up your mind to it. If you had sat in that cell for fourteen days making up your mind to it, you would understand that I'm not in the humor to be gaped at while youre trying to persuade yourself that it can't be real. These things really do happen to real people every day; and you read about them in the papers and think it's all right. Well, theyve happened to me: thats all.

KNOX [*feeble-forcible*] But they shouldnt have happened to you. Dont you know that?

MARGARET. They shouldnt happen to anybody, I suppose. But they do. [*Rising impatiently*] And really I'd rather go out and assault another policeman and go back to Holloway than keep talking round and round it like this. If youre going to turn me out of the house, turn me out: the sooner I go the better.

DUVALLET [*rising quickly*] That is impossible, mademoiselle. Your father has his position to consider. To turn his daughter out of doors would ruin him socially.

KNOX. Oh, youve put her up to that, have you? And where did you come in, may I ask?

DUVALLET. I came in at your invitation – at your amiable insistence, in fact, not at my own. But you need have no anxiety on my account. I was concerned in the regrettable incident which led to your daughter's incarceration. I got a fortnight without the option of a fine on the ridiculous ground that I ought to have struck the policeman with my fist. I should have done so with pleasure had I known; but, as it was, I struck him on the ear with my boot – a magnificent *moulinet*, I must say – and was informed that I had been guilty of an act of cowardice, but that for the sake of the *entente cordiale* I should be dealt with leniently. Yet Miss Knox, who used her fist, got a month, but with the option of a fine. I did not know this until I was released, when my first act was to pay the forty shillings. And here we are.

MRS KNOX. You ought to pay the gentleman the fine, Jo.

KNOX [*reddening*] Oh, certainly. [*He takes out some money*].

DUVALLET. Oh please! it does not matter. [*Knox hands him two sovereigns*]. If you insist – [*he pockets them*]. Thank you.

MARGARET. I'm ever so much obliged to you, Monsieur Duvallet.

DUVALLET. Can I be of any further assistance, mademoiselle?

MARGARET. I think you had better leave us to fight it out, if you dont mind.

DUVALLET. Perfectly. Madame [*bow*] – Mademoiselle [*bow*] – Monsieur [*bow*] – [*He goes out*].

MRS KNOX. Dont ring, Jo. See the gentleman out yourself.

Knox hastily sees Duvallet out. Mother and daughter sit looking forlornly at one another without saying a word. Mrs Knox slowly sits down. Margaret follows her example. They look at one another again. Mr Knox returns.

KNOX [*shortly and sternly*] Amelia: this is your job. [*To Margaret*] I leave you to your mother. I shall have my own say in the matter when I hear what you have to say to her. [*He goes out, solemn and offended*].

MARGARET [*with a bitter little laugh*] Just what the Suffraget said to me in Holloway. He throws the job on you.

MRS KNOX [*reproachfully*] Margaret!

MARGARET. You know it's true.

MRS KNOX. Margaret: if youre going to be hardened about it, theres no use my saying anything.

MARGARET. I'm not hardened, mother. But I cant talk nonsense about it. You see, it's all real to me. Ive suffered it. Ive been shoved and bullied. Ive had my arms twisted. Ive been made to scream with pain in other ways. Ive been flung into a filthy cell with a lot of other poor wretches as if I were a sack of coals being emptied into a cellar. And the only difference between me and the others was that I hit back. Yes I did. And I did worse. I wasnt ladylike. I cursed. I called names. I heard words that I didnt even know that I knew, coming out of my mouth just as if somebody else had spoken them. The policeman repeated them in court. The magistrate said he could hardly believe it. The policeman held out his hand with his two teeth in it that I knocked out. I said it was all right; that I had heard myself using those words quite distinctly; and that I had taken the good conduct prize for three years running at school. The poor old gentleman put me back for the missionary to find out who I was, and to ascertain the state of my mind. I wouldnt tell, of course, for your sakes at home here; and I wouldnt say I was sorry, or apologize to the policeman, or compensate him or anything of that sort. I wasnt sorry. The one thing that gave me any satisfaction was getting in that smack on his mouth; and I said so. So the missionary reported that I seemed hardened and that no doubt I would tell who I was after a day in prison. Then I was sentenced. So now you see I'm not a bit the sort of girl you thought me. I'm not a bit the sort of girl I thought myself. And I dont know what sort of person you really are, or what sort of person father really is. I wonder what he would say or do if he had an angry brute of a policeman twisting his arm with one hand and rushing him along by the nape of his neck with the other. He couldnt whirl his leg like a windmill and knock a policeman down by a glorious kick on the helmet. Oh, if theyd all fought as we two fought we'd have beaten them.

MRS KNOX. But how did it all begin?

MARGARET. Oh, I dont know. It was boat-race night, they said.

MRS KNOX. Boat-race night! But what had you to do with the boat race? You went to the great Salvation Festival at the Albert Hall with your aunt. She put you into the bus that passes the door. What made you get out of the bus?

MARGARET. I dont know. The meeting got on my nerves, somehow. It was the singing, I suppose: you know I love singing a good swinging hymn; and I felt it was ridiculous to go home in the bus after we had been singing so wonderfully about climbing up the golden stairs to heaven. I wanted more music – more happiness – more life. I wanted some comrade who felt as I did. I felt exalted: it seemed mean to be afraid of anything: after all, what could anyone do to me against my will? I suppose I was a little mad: at all events, I got out of the bus at Piccadilly Circus, because there was a lot of light and excitement there. I walked to Leicester Square; and went into a great theatre.

MRS KNOX [*horrified*] A theatre!

MARGARET. Yes, Lots of other women were going in alone. I had to pay five shillings.

MRS KNOX [*aghast*] Five shillings!

MARGARET [*apologetically*] It was a lot. It was very stuffy; and I didnt like the people much, because they didnt seem to be enjoying themselves; but the stage was splendid and the music lovely. I saw that Frenchman, Monsieur Duvallet, standing against a barrier, smoking a cigaret. He seemed quite happy; and he was nice and sailorlike. I went and stood beside him, hoping he would speak to me.

MRS KNOX [*gasps*] Margaret!

MARGARET [*continuing*] He did, just as if he had known me for years. We got on together like old friends. He asked me would I have some champagne; and I said it would cost too much, but that I would give anything for a dance. I longed to join the people on the stage and dance with them: one of them was the most beautiful dancer I ever saw. He told me he had come there to see her, and that when it was over we could go somewhere where there was dancing. So we went to a place where there was a band in a gallery and the floor cleared for dancing. Very few people danced: the women only wanted to shew off their dresses; but we danced and danced until a lot of them joined in. We got quite reckless; and we had champagne after all. I never enjoyed anything so much. But at last it got spoilt by the Oxford and Cambridge students up for the boat race. They got drunk; and they began to smash things; and the police came in. Then it was quite horrible. The students fought with the police; and the police suddenly got quite brutal, and began to throw everybody downstairs. They attacked the women, who were not doing anything, and treated them just as roughly as they had treated the students. Duvallet got indignant and remonstrated with a policeman, who was shoving a woman though she was going quietly as fast as she could. The policeman flung the woman through the door and then turned on Duvallet. It was then that Duvallet swung his leg like a windmill and knocked the policeman down. And then three policemen rushed at him and carried him out by the arms and legs face downwards. Two more attacked me and gave me a shove to the door. That quite maddened me. I just got in one good bang on the mouth of one of them. All the rest was dreadful. I was rushed through the streets to the police station. They kicked me with their knees; they twisted my arms; they taunted and insulted me; they called me vile names; and I told them what I thought of them, and provoked them to do their worst. Theres one good thing about being hard hurt: it makes you sleep. I slept in that filthy cell with all the other drunks sounder than I should have slept at home. I cant describe how I felt next morning: it was hideous; but the police were quite jolly; and everybody said it was a bit of English fun, and talked about last year's boat race night when it had been a great deal worse. I was black and blue and sick and wretched. But the strange thing was that I wasnt sorry; and I'm not sorry. And I dont feel that I did anything wrong, really. [*She rises and stretches her arms with a large liberating breath*] Now that it's all over I'm rather proud of it; though I know now that I'm not a lady; but whether thats because we're only shopkeepers, or because nobody's really a lady except when theyre treated like ladies, I dont know. [*She throws herself into a corner of the sofa*].

MRS KNOX [*lost in wonder*] But how could you bring yourself to do it, Margaret? I'm not blaming you: I only want to know. How could you bring yourself to do it?

MARGARET. I cant tell you. I dont understand it myself. The prayer meeting set me free, somehow. I should never have done it if it were not for the prayer meeting.

MRS KNOX [*deeply horrified*] Oh, dont say such a thing as that. I know that prayer can set us free; though you could never understand me when I told you so; but it sets us free for good, not for evil.

MARGARET. Then I suppose what I did was not evil; or else I was set free for evil as well as good. As father says, you cant have anything both ways at once. When I was at home and at school I was what you call good; but I wasnt free. And when I got free I was what most people would call not good. But I see no harm in what I did; though I see plenty in what other people did to me.

MRS KNOX. I hope you dont think yourself a heroine of romance.

MARGARET. On no. [*She sits down again at the table*]. I'm a heroine of reality, if you call me a heroine at all. And reality is pretty brutal, pretty filthy, when you come to grips with it. Yet it's glorious all the same. It's so real and satisfactory.

MRS KNOX. I dont like this spirit in you, Margaret. I dont like your talking to me in that tone.

MARGARET. It's no use, mother. I dont care for you and papa any the less; but I shall never get back to the old way of talking again. Ive made a sort of descent into hell –

MRS KNOX. Margaret! Such a word!

MARGARET. You should have heard all the words that were flying round that night. You should mix a little with people who dont know any other words. But when I said that about a descent into hell I was not swearing. I was in earnest, like a preacher.

MRS KNOX. A preacher utters them in a reverent tone of voice.

MARGARET. I know: the tone that shews they dont mean anything real to him. They usent to mean anything real to me. Now hell is as real to me as a turnip; and I suppose I shall always speak of it like that. Anyhow, Ive been there; and it seems to me now that nothing is worth doing but redeeming people from it.

MRS KNOX. They are redeemed already if they choose to believe it.

MARGARET. Whats the use of that if they dont choose to believe it? You dont believe it yourself, or you wouldnt pay policemen to twist their arms. Whats the good of pretending? Thats all our respectability is, pretending, pretending, pretending. Thank heaven Ive had it knocked out of me once for all!

MRS KNOX [*greatly agitated*] Margaret: dont talk like that. I cant bear to hear you talking wickedly. I can bear to hear the children of this world talking vainly and foolishly in the language of this world. But when I hear you justifying your wickedness in the words of grace, it's too horrible: it sounds like the devil making fun of religion. Ive tried to bring you up to learn the happiness of religion. Ive waited for you to find out that happiness is within ourselves and doesnt come from outward pleasures. Ive prayed oftener than you think that you might be enlightened. But if all my hopes and all my prayers are to come to this, that you mix up my very words and thoughts with the promptings of the devil, then I dont know what I shall do: I dont indeed: itll kill me.

MARGARET. You shouldnt have prayed for me to be enlightened if you didnt want me to be enlightened. If the truth were known, I suspect we all want our prayers to be answered only by halves: the agreeable halves. Your prayer didnt get answered by halves, mother. Youve got more than you bargained for in the way of enlightenment. I shall never be the same again. I shall never speak in the old way again. Ive been set free from this silly little hole of a house and all its pretences. I know now that I am stronger than you and papa. I havnt found that happiness of yours that is within yourself; but Ive found strength. For good or evil I am set free; and none of the things that used to hold me can hold me now.

Knox comes back, unable to bear his suspense.

KNOX. How long more are you going to keep me waiting, Amelia? Do you think I'm made of iron? Whats the girl done? What are we going to do?

MRS KNOX. She's beyond my control, Jo, and beyond yours. I cant even pray for her now; for I dont know rightly what to pray for.

KNOX. Dont talk nonsense, woman: is this a time for praying? Does anybody know? Thats what we have to consider now. If only we can keep it dark, I dont care for anything else.

MARGARET. Dont hope for that, father. Mind: I'll tell everybody. It ought to be told. It must be told.

KNOX. Hold your tongue, you young hussy; or go out of my house this instant.

MARGARET. I'm quite ready. [*She takes her hat and turns to the door*].

KNOX [*throwing himself in front of it*] Here! where are you going?

MRS KNOX [*rising*] You mustnt turn her out, Jo! I'll go with her if she goes.

KNOX. Who wants to turn her out? But is she going to ruin us? To let everybody know of her disgrace and shame? To tear me down from the position Ive made for myself and you by forty years hard struggling?

MARGARET. Yes: I'm going to tear it all down. It stands between us and everything. I'll tell everybody.

KNOX. Magsy, my child: dont bring down your father's hairs with sorrow to the grave. Theres only one thing I care about in the world: to keep this dark. I'm your father. I ask you here on my knees – in the dust, so to speak – not to let it out.

MARGARET. I'll tell everybody.

Knox collapses in despair. Mrs Knox tries to pray and cannot. Margaret stands inflexible.

ACT III

Again in the Gilbey's dining room. Afternoon. The table is not laid: it is draped in its ordinary cloth, with pen and ink, an exercise-book, and school-books on it. Bobby Gilbey is in the armchair, crouching over the fire, reading an illustrated paper. He is a pretty youth, of very surburban gentility, strong and manly enough by nature, but untrained and unsatisfactory, his parents having imagined that domestic restriction is what they call 'bringing up'. He has learnt nothing from it except a habit of evading it by deceit.

He gets up to ring the bell; then resumes his crouch. Juggins answers the bell.

BOBBY. Juggins.

JUGGINS. Sir?

BOBBY [*morosely sarcastic*] Sir be blowed!

JUGGINS [*cheerfully*] Not at all, sir.

BOBBY. I'm a gaol-bird: youre a respectable man.

JUGGINS. That doesnt matter, sir. Your father pays me to call you sir; and as I take the money, I keep my part of the bargain.

BOBBY. Would you call me sir if you wernt paid to do it?

JUGGINS. No, sir.

BOBBY. Ive been talking to Dora about you.

JUGGINS. Indeed, sir?

BOBBY. Yes, Dora says your name cant be Juggins, and that you have the manners of a gentleman. I always thought you hadnt any manners. Anyhow, your manners are different from the manners of a gentleman in my set.

JUGGINS. They would be, sir.

BOBBY. You dont feel disposed to be communicative on the subject of Dora's notion, I suppose.

JUGGINS. No, sir.

BOBBY [*throwing his paper on the floor and lifting his knees over the arm of the chair so as to turn towards the footman*] It was part of your bargain that you were to valet me a bit, wasnt it?

JUGGINS. Yes, sir.

BOBBY. Well, can you tell me the proper way to get out of an engagement to a girl without getting into a row for breach of promise?

JUGGINS. No, sir. You cant get out of an engagement without being sued for breach of promise if the lady wishes to be paid for her disappointment.

BOBBY. But it wouldnt be for her happiness to marry me when I dont really care for her.

JUGGINS. Women dont always marry for happiness, sir. They often marry because they wish to be married women and not old maids.

BOBBY. Then what am I to do?

JUGGINS. Marry her, sir, or take the consequences.

BOBBY [*jumping up*] Well, I wont marry her: thats flat. What would you do if you were in my place?

JUGGINS. I should tell the young lady that I found I couldnt fulfil my engagement.

BOBBY. But youd have to make some excuse, you know. I want to give it a gentlemanly turn: to say I'm not worthy of her, or something like that.

JUGGINS. That is not a gentlemanly turn, sir. Quite the contrary.

BOBBY. I dont see that at all. Do you mean that it's not exactly true?

JUGGINS. Not at all, sir.

BOBBY. I *can* say that no other girl can ever be to me what she's been. That would be quite true, because our circumstances have been rather exceptional; and she'll imagine I mean I'm fonder of her than I can ever be of anyone else. You see, Juggins, a gentleman has to think of a girl's feelings.

JUGGINS. If you wish to spare her feelings, sir, you can marry her. If you hurt her feelings by refusing, you had better not try to get credit for considerateness at the same time by pretending to spare them. She wont like it. And it will start an argument, of which you will get the worse.

BOBBY. But, you know, Im not really worthy of her.

JUGGINS. Probably she never supposed you were, sir.

BOBBY. Oh, I say, Juggins, you *are* a pessimist.

JUGGINS [*preparing to go*] Anything else, sir?

BOBBY [*querulously*] You havnt been much use. [*He wanders disconsolately across the room*]. You generally put me up to the correct way of doing things.

JUGGINS. I assure you, sir, theres no correct way of jilting. It's not correct in itself.

BOBBY [*hopefully*] I'll tell you what. I'll say I cant hold her to an engagement with a man whos been in quod. Thatll do it. [*He seats himself on the table, relieved and confident*].

JUGGINS. Very dangerous, sir. No woman will deny herself the romantic luxury of self-sacrifice and forgiveness when they take the form of doing something agreeable. She's almost sure to say that your misfortune will draw her closer to you.

BOBBY. What a nuisance! I dont know what to do. You know, Juggins, your cool simple-minded way of doing it wouldnt go down in Denmark Hill.

JUGGINS. I daresay not, sir. No doubt youd prefer to make it look like an act of self-sacrifice for her sake on your part, or provoke her to break the engagement herself. Both plans have been tried repeatedly, but never with success, as far as my knowledge goes.

BOBBY. You have a devilish cool way of laying down the law. You know, in my class you have to wrap up things a bit. Denmark Hill isnt Camberwell, you know.

JUGGINS. I have noticed, sir, that Denmark Hill thinks that the higher you go in the social scale, the less sincerity is allowed, and that only tramps and riff-raff are quite sincere. Thats a mistake. Tramps are often shameless; but theyre never sincere. Swells – if I may use that convenient name for the upper classes – play much more with their cards on the table. If you tell the young lady that you want to jilt her, and she calls you a pig, the tone of the transaction may leave much to be desired; but itll be less Camberwellian than if you say youre not worthy.

BOBBY. Oh, I cant make you understand, Juggins. The girl isnt a scullerymaid. I want to do it delicately.

JUGGINS. A mistake, sir, believe me, if you are not a born artist in that line. – Beg pardon, sir, I think I heard the bell. [*He goes out*].

Bobby, much perplexed, shoves his hands into his pockets, and comes off the table, staring disconsolately straight before him; then goes reluctantly to his books, and sits down to write. Juggins returns.

JUGGINS [*announcing*] Miss Knox.

Margaret comes in. Juggins withdraws.

MARGARET. Still grinding away for that Society of Arts examination, Bobby? Youll never pass.

BOBBY [*rising*] No: I was just writing to you.

MARGARET. What about?

BOBBY. Oh, nothing. At least – How are you?

MARGARET [*passing round the other end of the table and putting down on it a copy of Lloyd's Weekly and her purse-bag*] Quite well, thank you. How did you enjoy Brighton?

BOBBY. Brighton! I wasnt at – Oh yes, of course, Oh, pretty well. Is your aunt all right?

MARGARET. My aunt! I suppose so. I havent seen her for a month.

BOBBY. I thought you were down staying with her.

MARGARET. Oh! was that what they told you?

BOBBY. Yes. Why? Wernt you really?

MARGARET. No. Ive something to tell you. Sit down and lets be comfortable.

She sits on the edge of the table. He sits beside her, and puts his arm wearily round her waist.

MARGARET. You neednt do that if you dont like, Bobby. Suppose we get off duty for the day, just to see what it's like.

BOBBY. Off duty? What do you mean?

MARGARET. You know very well what I mean. Bobby: did you ever care one little scrap for me in that sort of way? Dont funk answering: *I* dont care a bit for you – that way.

BOBBY [*removing his arm rather huffily*] I beg your pardon, I'm sure. I thought you did.

MARGARET. Well, did you? Come! Dont be mean. Ive owned up. You can put it all on me if you like, but I dont believe you care any more than I do.

BOBBY. You mean weve been shoved into it rather by the pars and mars.

MARGARET. Yes.

BOBBY. Well, it's not that I dont care for you: in fact, no girl can ever be to me exactly what you are; but weve been brought up so much together that it feels more like brother and sister than – well, than the other thing, doesnt it?

MARGARET. Just so. How did you find out the difference?

BOBBY [*blushing*] Oh, I say!

MARGARET. I found out from a Frenchman.

BOBBY. Oh, I say! [*He comes off the table in his consternation*].

MARGARET. Did you learn it from a Frenchwoman? You know you must have learnt it from somebody.

BOBBY. Not a Frenchwoman. She's quite a nice woman. But she's been rather unfortunate. The daughter of a clergyman.

MARGARET [*startled*] Oh, Bobby! That sort of woman!

BOBBY. What sort of woman?

MARGARET. You dont believe she's really a clergyman's daughter, do you, you silly boy? It's a stock joke.

BOBBY. Do you mean to say you dont believe me?

MARGARET. No: I mean to say I dont believe her.

BOBBY [*curious and interested, resuming his seat on the table beside her*] What do you know about her? What do you know about all this sort of thing?

MARGARET. What sort of thing, Bobby?

BOBBY. Well, about life.

MARGARET. Ive lived a lot since I saw you last. I wasnt at my aunt's. All that time that you were in Brighton, I mean.

BOBBY. I wasnt at Brighton, Meg. I'd better tell you: youre bound to find out sooner or later. [*He begins his confession humbly, avoiding her gaze*]. Meg: it's rather awful: youll think me no end of a beast. Ive been in prison.

MARGARET. You!

BOBBY. Yes, me. For being drunk and assaulting the police.

MARGARET. Do you mean to say that you – oh! this is a letdown for me. [*She comes off the table and drops, disconsolate, into a chair at the end of it furthest from the hearth*].

BOBBY. Of course I couldnt hold you to our engagement after that. I was writing to you to break it off. [*He also descends from the table and makes slowly for the hearth*]. You must think me an utter rotter.

MARGARET. Oh, has everybody been in prison for being drunk and assaulting the police? How long were you in?

BOBBY. A fortnight.

MARGARET. Thats what I was in for.

BOBBY. What are you talking about? In where?

MARGARET. In quod.

BOBBY. But I'm serious: I'm not rotting. Really and truly –

MARGARET. What did you do to the copper?

BOBBY. Nothing, absolutely nothing. He exaggerated grossly. I only laughed at him.

MARGARET [*jumping up, triumphant*] Ive beaten you hollow. I knocked out two of his teeth. Ive got one of them. He sold it to me for ten shillings.

BOBBY. Now please do stop fooling, Meg. I tell you I'm not rotting. [*He sits down in the armchair, rather sulkily*].

MARGARET [*taking up the copy of Lloyd's Weekly and going to him*] And I tell you I'm not either. Look! Heres a report of it. The daily papers are no good; but the Sunday papers are splendid. [*She sits on the arm of the chair*]. See! [*Reading*] 'Hardened at Eighteen. A quietly dressed, respectable-looking girl who refuses her name' – thats me.

BOBBY [*pausing a moment in his perusal*] Do you mean to say that you went on the loose out of pure devilment?

MARGARET. I did no harm. I went to see a lovely dance. I picked up a nice man and went to have a dance myself. I cant imagine anything more innocent and more happy. All the bad part was done by other people: they did it out of pure devilment if you like. Anyhow, here we are, two gaol-birds, Bobby, disgraced forever. Isnt it a relief?

BOBBY [*rising stiffly*] But you know, it's not the same for a girl. A man may do things a woman maynt. [*He stands on the hearthrug with his back to the fire*].

MARGARET. Are you scandalized, Bobby?

BOBBY. Well, you cant expect me to approve of it, can you, Meg? I never thought you were that sort of girl.

MARGARET [*rising indignantly*] I'm not. You mustnt pretend to think that *I*'m a clergyman's daughter, Bobby.

BOBBY. I wish you wouldnt chaff about that. Dont forget the row you got into for letting out that you admired Juggins [*she turns her back on him quickly*] – a footman! And what about the Frenchman?

MARGARET [*facing him again*] I know nothing about the Frenchman except that he's a very nice fellow and can swing his leg round like the hand of a clock and knock a policeman down with it. He was in Wormwood Scrubs with you. I was in Holloway.

BOBBY. It's all very well to make light of it, Meg; but this is a bit thick, you know.

MARGARET. Do you feel you couldnt marry a woman whos been in prison.

BOBBY [*hastily*] No. I never said that. It might even give a woman a greater claim on a man. Any girl, if she were thoughtless and a bit on, perhaps, might get into a scrape. Anyone who really understood her character could see there was no harm in it. But youre not the larky sort. At least you usent to be.

MARGARET. I'm not; and I never will be. [*She walks straight up to him*]. I didnt do it for a lark, Bob: I did it out of the very depths of my nature. I did it because I'm that sort of person. I did it in one of my religious fits. I'm hardened at eighteen, as they say. So what about the match, now?

BOBBY. Well, I dont think you can fairly hold me to it, Meg. Of course it would be ridiculous for me to set up to be shocked, or anything of that sort. I cant afford to throw stones at anybody; and I dont pretend to. I can understand a lark; I can forgive a slip; as long as it is understood that it is only a lark or a slip. But to go on the loose on principle; to talk about religion in connection with it; to – to – well, Meg, I do find that a bit thick, I must say. I hope youre not in earnest when you talk that way.

MARGARET. Bobby: youre no good. No good to me, anyhow.

BOBBY [*huffed*] I'm sorry, Miss Knox.

MARGARET. Goodbye, Mr Gilbey. [*She turns on her heel and goes to the other end of the table*]. I suppose you wont introduce me to the clergyman's daughter.

BOBBY. I dont think she'd like it. There are limits, after all. [*He sits down at the table, as if to resume work at his books: a hint to her to go*].

MARGARET [*on her way to the door*] Ring the bell, Bobby; and tell Juggins to shew me out.

BOBBY [*reddening*] I'm not a cad, Meg.

MARGARET [*coming to the table*] Then do something nice to prevent us feeling mean about this afterwards. Youd better kiss me. You neednt ever do it again.

BOBBY. If I'm no good, I dont see what fun it would be for you.

MARGARET. Oh, it'd be no fun. If I wanted what you call fun, I should ask the Frenchman to kiss me – or Juggins.

BOBBY [*rising and retreating to the hearth*] Oh, dont be disgusting, Meg. Dont be low.

MARGARET [*determinedly, preparing to use force*] No, I'll make you kiss me, just to punish you. [*She seizes his wrist; pulls him off his balance; and gets her arm round his neck*].

BOBBY. No. Stop. Leave go, will you.

Juggins appears at the door.

JUGGINS. Miss Delaney, sir. [*Dora comes in. Juggins goes out. Margaret hastily releases Bobby, and goes to the other side of the room*].

DORA [*through the door, to the departing Juggins*] Well, you are a Juggins to shew me up when theres company. [*To Margaret and Bobby*] It's all right, dear: all right, old man: I'll wait in Juggins's pantry till youre disengaged.

MARGARET. Dont you know me?

DORA [*coming to the middle of the room and looking at her very attentively*] Why, it's never No. 406!

MARGARET. Yes it is.

DORA. Well, I should never have known you out of the uniform. How did you get out? You were doing a month, wernt you?

MARGARET. My bloke paid the fine the day he got out himself.

DORA. A real gentleman! [*Pointing to Bobby, who is staring open-mouthed*] Look at him! He cant take it in.

BOBBY. I suppose you made her acquaintance in prison, Meg. But when it comes to talking about blokes and all that – well!

MARGARET. Oh, Ive learnt the language; and I like it. It's another barrier broken down.

BOBBY. It's not so much the language, Meg. But I think [*he looks at Dora and stops*].

MARGARET [*suddenly dangerous*] What do you think, Bobby?

DORA. He thinks you oughtnt to be so free with me, dearie. It does him credit: he always was a gentleman, you know.

MARGARET. Does him credit! To insult you like that! Bobby: say that that wasnt what you meant.

BOBBY. I didnt say it was.

MARGARET. Well, deny that it was.

BOBBY. No. I wouldnt have said it in front of Dora; but I do think it's not quite the same thing my knowing her and you knowing her.

DORA. Of course it isnt, old man. [*To Margaret*] I'll just trot off and come back in half an hour. You two can make it up together. I'm really not fit company for you, dearie: I couldnt live up to you. [*She turns to go*].

MARGARET. Stop. Do you believe he could live up to me?

DORA. Well, I'll never say anything to stand between a girl and a respectable marriage, or to stop a decent lad from settling himself. I have a conscience; though I maynt be as particular as some.

MARGARET. You seem to me to be a very decent sort; and Bobby's behaving like a skunk.

BOBBY [*much ruffled*] Nice language that!

DORA. Well, dearie, men have to do some awfully mean things to keep up their respectability. But you cant blame them for that, can you? Ive met Bobby walking with his mother; and of course he cut me dead. I wont pretend I liked it; but what could he do, poor dear?

MARGARET. And now he wants me to cut you dead to keep him in countenance. Well, I shant: not if my whole family were there. But I'll cut him dead if he doesnt treat you properly. [*To Bobby, with a threatening move in his direction*] I'll educate you, you young beast.

BOBBY [*furious, meeting her half-way*] Who are you calling a young beast?

MARGARET. You.

DORA [*peacemaking*] Now, dearies!

BOBBY. If you dont take care, youll get your fat head jolly well clouted.

MARGARET. If you dont take care, the policeman's tooth will be the beginning of a collection.

DORA. Now, loveys, be good.

Bobby, lost to all sense of adult dignity, puts out his tongue at Margaret. Margaret, equally furious, catches his protended countenance a box on the cheek. He hurls himself on her. They wrestle.

BOBBY. Cat! I'll teach you.

MARGARET. Pig! Beast! [*She forces him backwards on the table*]. Now where are you?

DORA [*calling*] Juggins, Juggins. Theyll murder one another.

JUGGINS [*throwing open the door, and announcing*] Monsieur Duvallet.

Duvallet enters. Sudden cessation of hostilities, and dead silence. The combatants separate by the whole width of the room. Juggins withdraws.

DUVALLET. I fear I derange you.

MARGARET. Not at all. Bobby: you really are a beast: Monsieur Duvallet will think I'm always fighting.

DUVALLET. Practising jujitsu or the new Iceland wrestling. Admirable, Miss Knox. The athletic young Englishwoman is an example to all Europe. [*Indicating Bobby*] Your instructor, no doubt. Monsieur – [*he bows*].

BOBBY [*bowing awkwardly*] How d'y' do?

MARGARET [*to Bobby*] I'm so sorry, Bobby: I asked Monsieur Duvallet to call for me here; and I forgot to tell you. [*Introducing*] Monsieur Duvallet: Miss Four hundred and seven. Mr Bobby Gilbey. [*Duvallet bows*]. I really dont know how to explain our relationships. Bobby and I are like brother and sister.

DUVALLET. Perfectly. I noticed it.

MARGARET. Bobby and Miss – Miss –

DORA. Delaney, dear. [*To Duvallet, bewitchingly*] Darling Dora to real friends.

MARGARET. Bobby and Dora are – are – well, not brother and sister.

DUVALLET [*with redoubled comprehension*] PERfectly.

MARGARET. Bobby has spent the last fortnight in prison. You dont mind, do you?

DUVALLET. No, naturally. *I* have spent the last fortnight in prison.

The conversation drops. Margaret renews it with an effort.

MARGARET. Dora has spent the last fortnight in prison.

DUVALLET. Quite so. I felicitate Mademoiselle on her enlargement.

DORA. *Trop merci*, as they say in Boulogne. No call to be stiff with one another, have we?

Juggins comes in.

JUGGINS. Beg pardon, sir. Mr and Mrs Gilbey are coming up the street.

DORA. Let me absquatulate [*making for the door*].

JUGGINS. If you wish to leave without being seen, you had better step into my pantry and leave afterwards.

DORA. Rightho! [*She bursts into song*]

> Hide me in the meat safe til the cop goes by.
> Hum the dear old music as his step draws nigh.

[*She goes out on tiptoe*].

MARGARET. I wont stay here if she has to hide. I'll keep her company in the pantry. [*She follows Dora*].

BOBBY. Lets all go. We cant have any fun with the Mar here. I say, Juggins: you can give us tea in the pantry, cant you?

JUGGINS. Certainly, sir.

BOBBY. Right. Say nothing to my mother. You dont mind, Mr Doovalley, do you?

DUVALLET. I shall be charmed.

BOBBY. Right you are. Come along. [*At the door*] Oh, by the way, Juggins, fetch down that concertina from my room, will you?

JUGGINS. Yes, sir. [*Bobby goes out. Duvallet follows him to the door*]. You understand, sir, that Miss Knox is a lady absolutely *comme il faut*?

DUVALLET. Perfectly. But the other?

JUGGINS. The other, sir, may be both charitably and accurately described in your native idiom as a daughter of joy.

DUVALLET. It is what I thought. These English domestic interiors are very interesting. [*He goes out, followed by Juggins*].

Presently Mr and Mrs Gilbey come in. They take their accustomed places: he on the hearthrug, she at the colder end of the table.

MRS GILBEY. Did you smell scent in the hall, Rob?

GILBEY. No, I didnt. And I dont want to smell it. Dont you go looking for trouble, Maria.

MRS GILBEY [*snuffing up the perfumed atmosphere*] She's been here. [*Gilbey rings the bell*]. What are you ringing for? Are you going to ask?

GILBEY. No, I'm not going to ask. Juggins said this morning he wanted to speak to me. If he likes to tell me, let him; but I'm not going to ask; and dont you either. [*Juggins appears at the door*]. You said you wanted to say something to me.

JUGGINS. When it would be convenient to you, sir.

GILBEY. Well, what is it?

MRS GILBEY. Oh, Juggins, we're expecting Mr and Mrs Knox to tea.

GILBEY. He knows that. [*He sits down. Then, to Juggins*] What is it?

JUGGINS [*advancing to the middle of the table*] Would it inconvenience you, sir, if I were to give you a month's notice?

GILBEY [*taken aback*] What! Why! Aint you satisfied?

JUGGINS. Perfectly, sir. It is not that I want to better myself, I assure you.

GILBEY. Well, what do you want to leave for, then? Do you want to worse yourself?

JUGGINS. No, sir. Ive been well treated in your most comfortable establishment; and I should be greatly distressed if you or Mrs Gilbey were to interpret my notice as an expression of dissatisfaction.

GILBEY [*paternally*] Now you listen to me, Juggins. I'm an older man than you. Dont you throw out dirty water til you get in fresh. Dont get too big for your boots. Youre like all servants nowadays: you think youve only to hold up your finger to get the pick of half a dozen jobs. But you wont be treated everywhere as youre treated here. In bed every night before eleven; hardly a ring at the door except on Mrs Gilbey's day once a month; and no other manservant to interfere with you. It may be a bit quiet perhaps; but youre past the age of adventure. Take my advice: think over it. You suit me; and I'm prepared to make it suit you if youre dissatisfied – in reason, you know.

JUGGINS. I realize my advantages, sir; but Ive private reasons –

GILBEY [*cutting him short angrily and retiring to the hearthrug in dudgeon*] Oh, I know. Very well: go. The sooner the better.

MRS GILBEY. Oh, not until we're suited. He must stay his month.

GILBEY [*sarcastic*] Do you want to lose him his character, Maria? Do you think I dont see what it is? We're prison folk now. Weve been in the police court. [*To Juggins*] Well, I suppose you know your own business best. I take your notice: you can go when your month is up, or sooner, if you like.

JUGGINS. Believe me, sir –

GILBEY. Thats enough: I dont want any excuses. I dont blame you. You can go downstairs now, if youve nothing else to trouble me about.

JUGGINS. I really cant leave it at that, sir. I assure you Ive no objection to young Mr Gilbey's going to prison. You may do six months yourself, sir, and welcome, without a word of remonstrance from me. I'm leaving solely because my brother, who has suffered a bereavement, and feels lonely, begs me to spend a few months with him until he gets over it.

GILBEY. And is he to keep you all that time? or are you to spend your savings in comforting him? Have some sense, man: how can you afford such things?

JUGGINS. My brother can afford to keep me, sir. The truth is, he objects to my being in service.

GILBEY. Is that any reason why you should be dependent on him? Dont do it, Juggins: pay your own way like an honest lad; and dont eat your brother's bread while youre able to earn your own.

JUGGINS. There is sound sense in that, sir. But unfortunately it is a tradition in my family that the younger brothers should spunge to a considerable extent on the eldest.

GILBEY. Then the sooner that tradition is broken the better, my man.

JUGGINS. A Radical sentiment, sir. But an excellent one.

GILBEY. Radical! What do you mean? Dont you begin to take liberties, Juggins, now that you know we're loth to part with you. Your brother isnt a duke, you know.

JUGGINS. Unfortunately, he is, sir.

GILBEY. } *together* { What!
MRS GILBEY. } { Juggins!

JUGGINS. Excuse me, sir: the bell. [*He goes out*].

GILBEY [*overwhelmed*] Maria: did you understand him to say his brother was a duke?

MRS GILBEY. Fancy his condescending! Perhaps if youd offer to raise his wages and treat him as one of the family, he'd stay.

GILBEY. And have my own servant above me! Not me. What's the world coming to? Heres Bobby and –

JUGGINS [*entering and announcing*] Mr and Mrs Knox.

The Knoxes come in. Juggins takes two chairs from the wall and places them at the table, between the host and hostess. Then he withdraws.

MRS GILBEY [*to Mrs Knox*] How are you, dear?

MRS KNOX. Nicely, thank you. Good evening, Mr Gilbey. [*They shake hands; and she takes the chair nearest Mrs Gilbey. Mr Knox takes the other chair*].

GILBEY [*sitting down*] I was just saying, Knox, What is the world coming to?

KNOX [*appealing to his wife*] What was I saying myself only this morning?

MRS KNOX. This is a strange time. I was never one to talk about the end of the world; but look at the things that have happened!

KNOX. Earthquakes!

GILBEY. San Francisco!

MRS GILBEY. Jamaica!

KNOX. Martinique!

GILBEY. Messina!

MRS GILBEY. The plague in China!

MRS KNOX. The floods in France!

GILBEY. My Bobby in Wormwood Scrubs!

KNOX. Margaret in Holloway!

GILBEY. And now my footman tells me his brother's a duke!

KNOX. } { No!
MRS KNOX. } { Whats that?

GILBEY. Just before he let you in. A duke! Here has everything been respectable from the beginning of the world, as you may say, to the present day; and all of a sudden everything is turned upside down.

MRS KNOX. It's like in the book of Revelations. But I do say that when people have happiness within themselves, all the earthquakes, all the floods, and all the prisons in the world cant make them really unhappy.

KNOX. It isnt alone the curious things that are happening, but the unnatural way people are taking them. Why, theres Margaret been in prison, and she hasnt time to go to all the invitations she's had from people that never asked her before.

GILBEY. I never knew we could live without being respectable.

MRS GILBEY. Oh, Rob, what a thing to say! Who says we're not respectable?

GILBEY. Well, it's not what I call respectable to have your children in and out of jail.

KNOX. Oh, come, Gilbey! we're not tramps because weve had, as it were, an accident.

GILBEY. It's no use, Knox: look it in the face. Did I ever tell you my father drank?

KNOX. No. But I knew it. Simmons told me.

GILBEY. Yes: he never could keep his mouth quiet: he told me your aunt was a kleptomaniac.

MRS KNOX. It wasnt true, Mr Gilbey. She used to pick up handkerchiefs if she saw them lying about; but you might trust her with untold silver.

GILBEY. My Uncle Phil was a teetotaler. My father used to say to me: Rob, he says, dont you ever have a weakness. If you find one getting a hold on you, make a merit of it, he says. Your Uncle Phil doesnt like spirits; and he makes a merit of it, and is chairman of the Blue Ribbon Committee. I do like spirits; and I make a merit of it, and I'm the King Cockatoo of the Convivial Cockatoos. Never put yourself in the wrong, he says. I used to boast about what a good boy Bobby was. Now I swank about what a dog he is; and it pleases people just as well. What a world it is!

KNOX. It turned my blood cold at first to hear Margaret telling people about Holloway; but it goes down better than her singing used to.

MRS KNOX. I never thought she sang right after all those lessons we paid for.

GILBEY. Lord, Knox, it was lucky you and me got let in together. I tell you straight, if it hadnt been for Bobby's disgrace, I'd have broke up the firm.

KNOX. I shouldnt have blamed you: I'd have done the same only for Margaret. Too much straitlacedness narrows a man's mind. Talking of that, what about those hygienic corset advertisements that Vines & Jackson want us to put in the window? I told Vines they wernt decent and we couldnt shew them in our shop. I was pretty high with him. But what am I to say to him now if he comes and throws this business in our teeth?

GILBEY. Oh, put em in. We may as well go it a bit now.

MRS GILBEY. Youve been going it quite far enough, Rob. [*To Mrs*

Knox] He wont get up in the mornings now: he that was always out of bed at seven to the tick!

MRS KNOX. You hear that, Jo? [*To Mrs Gilbey*] He's taken to whisky and soda. A pint a week! And the beer the same as before!

KNOX. Oh, dont preach, old girl.

MRS KNOX [*to Mrs Gilbey*] Thats a new name he's got for me. [*To Knox*] I tell you, Jo, this doesnt sit well on you. You may call it preaching if you like; but it's the truth for all that. I say that if youve happiness within yourself, you dont need to see it outside, spending money on drink and theatres and bad company, and being miserable after all. You can sit at home and be happy; and you can work and be happy. If you have that in you, the spirit will set you free to do what you want and guide you to do right. But if you havnt got it, then youd best be respectable and stick to the ways that are marked out for you; for youve nothing else to keep you straight.

KNOX [*angrily*] And is a man never to have a bit of fun? See whats come of it with your daughter! She was to be content with your happiness that youre always talking about; and how did the spirit guide her? To a month's hard for being drunk and assaulting the police. Did *I* ever assault the police?

MRS KNOX. You wouldnt have the courage. I dont blame the girl.

MRS GILBEY. } Oh, Maria! What are you saying?
GILBEY. } What! And you so pious!

MRS KNOX. She went where the spirit guided her. And what harm there was in it she knew nothing about.

GILBEY. Oh, come, Mrs Knox! Girls are not so innocent as all that.

MRS KNOX. I dont say she was ignorant. But I do say that she didnt know what we know: I mean the way certain temptations get a sudden hold that no goodness nor self-control is any use against. She was saved from that, and had a rough lesson too; and I say it was no earthly protection that did that. But dont think, you two men, that youll be protected if you make what she did an excuse to go and do as youd like to do if it wasnt for the fear of losing your characters. The spirit wont guide you, because it isnt in you; and it never has been: not in either of you.

GILBEY [*with ironic humility*] I'm sure I'm obliged to you for your good opinion, Mrs Knox.

MRS KNOX. Well, I will say for you, Mr Gilbey, that youre better than my man here. He's a bitter hard heathen, is my Jo, God help me! [*She begins to cry quietly*].

KNOX. Now, dont take on like that, Amelia. You know I always gave in to you that you were right about religion. But one of us had to think of other things, or we'd have starved, we and the child.

MRS KNOX. How do you know youd have starved? All the other things might have been added unto you.

GILBEY. Come, Mrs Knox, dont tell me Knox is a sinner. I know better. I'm sure youd be the first to be sorry if anything was to happen to him.

KNOX [*bitterly to his wife*] Youve always had some grudge against me; and nobody but yourself can understand what it is.

MRS KNOX. I wanted a man who had that happiness within himself. You made me think you had it; but it was nothing but being in love with me.

MRS GILBEY. And do you blame him for that?

MRS KNOX. I blame nobody. But let him not think he can walk by his own light. I tell him that if he gives up being respectable he'll go right down to the bottom of the hill. He has no powers inside himself to keep him steady; so let him cling to the powers outside him.

KNOX [*rising angrily*] Who wants to give up being respectable? All this for a pint of whisky that lasted a week! How long would it have lasted Simmons, I wonder?

MRS KNOX [*gently*] Oh, well, say no more, Jo. I wont plague you about it. [*He sits down*]. You never did understand; and you never will. Hardly anybody understands: even Margaret didnt til she went to prison. She does now; and I shall have a companion in the house after all these lonely years.

KNOX [*beginning to cry*] I did all I could to make you happy. I never said a harsh word to you.

GILBEY [*rising indignantly*] What right have you to treat a man like that? an honest respectable husband? as if he were dirt under your feet?

KNOX. Let her alone, Gilbey. [*Gilbey sits down, but mutinously*].

MRS KNOX. Well, you gave me all you could, Jo; and if it wasnt what I wanted, that wasnt your fault. But I'd rather have you as you were than since you took to whisky and soda.

KNOX. I dont want any whisky and soda. I'll take the pledge if you like.

MRS KNOX. No: you shall have your beer because you like it. The whisky was only brag. And if you and me are to remain friends, Mr Gilbey, youll get up tomorrow morning at seven.

GILBEY [*defiantly*] Damme if I will! There!

MRS KNOX [*with gentle pity*] How do you know, Mr Gilbey, what youll do tomorrow morning?

GILBEY. Why shouldnt I know? Are we children not to be let do what we like, and our own sons and daughters kicking their heels all over the place? [*To Knox*] I was never one to interfere between man and wife, Knox; but if Maria started ordering me about like that –

MRS GILBEY. Now dont be naughty, Rob. You know you mustnt set yourself up against religion.

GILBEY. Whos setting himself up against religion?

MRS KNOX. It doesnt matter whether you set yourself up against it or not, Mr Gilbey. If it sets itself up against you, youll have to go the appointed way: it's no use quarrelling about it with me that am as great a sinner as yourself.

GILBEY. Oh, indeed! And who told you I was a sinner?

MRS GILBEY. Now, Rob, you know we are all sinners. What else is religion?

GILBEY. I say nothing against religion. I suppose we're all sinners, in a manner of speaking; but I dont like to have it thrown at me as if I'd really done anything.

MRS GILBEY. Mrs Knox is speaking for your good, Rob.

GILBEY. Well, I dont like to be spoken to for my good. Would anybody like it?

MRS KNOX. Dont take offence where none is meant, Mr Gilbey. Talk about something else. No good ever comes of arguing about such things among the like of us.

KNOX. The like of us! Are you throwing it in our teeth that your people were in the wholesale and thought Knox and Gilbey wasnt good enough for you?

MRS KNOX. No, Jo: you know I'm not. What better were my people than yours, for all their pride? But Ive noticed it all my life: we're ignorant. We dont really know whats right and whats wrong. We're all right as long as things go on the way they always did. We bring our children up just as we were brought up; and we go to church or chapel just as our parents did; and we say what everybody says; and it goes on all right until something out of the way happens: theres a family quarrel, or one of the children goes wrong, or a father takes to drink, or an aunt goes mad, or one of us finds ourselves doing something we never thought we'd want to do. And then you know what happens; complaints and quarrels and huff and offence and bad language and bad temper and regular bewilderment as if Satan possessed us all. We find out then that with all our respectability and piety, weve no real religion and no way of telling right from wrong. Weve nothing but our habits; and when theyre upset, where are we? Just like Peter in the storm trying to walk on the water and finding he couldnt.

MRS GILBEY [*piously*] Aye! He found out, didnt he?

GILBEY [*reverently*] I never denied that youve a great intellect, Mrs Knox –

MRS KNOX. Oh, get along with you, Gilbey, if you begin talking about my intellect. Give us some tea, Maria. Ive said my say; and I'm sure I beg the company's pardon for being so long about it, and so disagreeable.

MRS GILBEY. Ring, Rob. [*Gilbey rings*]. Stop. Juggins will think we're ringing for him.

GILBEY [*appalled*] It's too late. I rang before I thought of it.

MRS GILBEY. Step down and apologize, Rob.

KNOX. Is it him that you said was brother to a –

Juggins comes in with the tea-tray. All rise. He takes the tray to Mrs Gilbey.

GILBEY. I didnt mean to ask you to do this, Mr Juggins. I wasnt thinking when I rang.

MRS GILBEY [*trying to take the tray from him*] Let me, Juggins.

JUGGINS. Please sit down, madam. Allow me to discharge my duties just as usual, sir. I assure you that is the correct thing.

They sit down, ill at ease, whilst he places the tray on the table. He then goes out for the curate.

KNOX [*lowering his voice*] Is this all right, Gilbey? Anybody may be the son of a duke, you know. Is he legitimate?

GILBEY. Good Lord! I never thought of that.

Juggins returns with the cakes. They regard him with suspicion.

GILBEY [*whispering to Knox*] You ask him.

KNOX [*to Juggins*] Just a word with you, my man. Was your mother married to your father?

JUGGINS. I believe so, sir. I cant say from personal knowledge. It was before my time.

GILBEY. Well but look here you know – [*he hesitates*].

JUGGINS. Yes, sir?

KNOX. I know whatll clinch it, Gilbey. You leave it to me. [*To Juggins*] Was your mother the duchess?

JUGGINS. Yes, sir. Quite correct, sir. I assure you. [*To Mrs Gilbey*] That is the milk, madam. [*She has mistaken the jugs*]. This is the water.

They stare at him in pitiable embarrassment.

MRS KNOX. What did I tell you? Heres something out of the common happening with a servant; and we none of us know how to behave.

JUGGINS. It's quite simple, madam. I'm a footman, and should be treated as a footman. [*He proceeds calmly with his duties, handing round cups of tea as Mrs Knox fills them*].

Shrieks of laughter from below stairs reach the ears of the company.

MRS GILBEY. Whats that noise? Is Master Bobby at home? I heard his laugh.

MRS KNOX. I'm sure I heard Margaret's.

GILBEY. Not a bit of it. It was that woman.

JUGGINS. I can explain, sir. I must ask you to excuse the liberty; but I'm entertaining a small party to tea in my pantry.

MRS GILBEY. But youre not entertaining Master Bobby?

JUGGINS. Yes, madam.

GILBEY. Whos with him?

JUGGINS. Miss Knox, sir.

GILBEY. Miss Knox! Are you sure? Is there anyone else?

JUGGINS. Only a French marine officer, sir, and – er – Miss Delaney. [*He places Gilbey's tea on the table before him*]. The lady that called about Master Bobby, sir.

KNOX. Do you mean to say theyre having a party all to themselves downstairs, and we having a party up here and knowing nothing about it?

JUGGINS. Yes, sir. I have to do a good deal of entertaining in the pantry for Master Bobby, sir.

GILBEY. Well, this is a nice state of things!

KNOX. Whats the meaning of it? What do they do it for?

JUGGINS. To enjoy themselves, sir, I should think.

MRS GILBEY. Enjoy themselves! Did ever anybody hear of such a thing?

GILBEY. Knox's daughter shewn into my pantry!

KNOX. Margaret mixing with a Frenchman and a footman – [*Suddenly realising that the footman is offering him cake*] She doesnt know about – about His Grace, you know.

MRS GILBEY. Perhaps she does. Does she, Mr Juggins?

JUGGINS. The other lady suspects me, madam. They call me Rudolph, or the Long Lost Heir.

MRS GILBEY. It's a much nicer name than Juggins. I think I'll call you by it, if you dont mind.

JUGGINS. Not at all, madam.

Roars of merriment from below.

GILBEY. Go and tell them to stop laughing. What right have they to make a noise like that?

JUGGINS. I asked them not to laugh so loudly, sir. But the French gentleman always sets them off again.

KNOX. Do you mean to tell me that my daughter laughs at a Frenchman's jokes?

GILBEY. We all know what French jokes are.

JUGGINS. Believe me: you do not, sir. The noise this afternoon has all been because the Frenchman said that the cat had whooping cough.

MRS GILBEY [*laughing heartily*] Well, I never!

GILBEY. Dont be a fool, Maria. Look here, Knox: we cant let this go on. People cant be allowed to behave like this.

KNOX. Just what I say.

A concertina adds its music to the revelry.

MRS GILBEY [*excited*] Thats the squiffer. He's bought it for her.

GILBEY. Well, of all the scandalous – [*Redoubled laughter from below*].

KNOX. I'll put a stop to this. [*He goes out to the landing and shouts*] Margaret! [*Sudden dead silence*]. Margaret, I say!

MARGARET'S VOICE. Yes, father. Shall we all come up? We're dying to.

KNOX. Come up and be ashamed of yourselves, behaving like wild Indians.

DORA'S VOICE [*screaming*] Oh! oh! oh! Dont, Bobby. Now – Oh! [*In headlong flight she dashes into and right across the room, breathless, and slightly abashed by the company*]. I beg your pardon, Mrs Gilbey, for coming in like that; but whenever I go upstairs in front of Bobby, he pretends it's a cat biting my ankles; and I just must scream.

Bobby and Margaret enter rather more shyly, but evidently in high spirits. Bobby places himself near his father, on the hearthrug, and presently slips down into the armchair.

MARGARET. How do you do, Mrs Gilbey? [*She puts herself behind her mother*].

Duvallet comes in behaving himself perfectly. Knox follows.

MARGARET. Oh – let me introduce. My friend Lieutenant Duvallet. Mrs Gilbey. Mr Gilbey.

Duvallet bows and sits down on Mr Knox's left, Juggins placing a chair for him.

DORA. Now, Bobby: introduce me: theres a dear.

BOBBY [*a little nervous about it; but trying to keep up his spirits*] Miss Delaney: Mr and Mrs Knox. [*Knox, as he resumes his seat, acknowledges the introduction suspiciously. Mrs Knox bows gravely, looking keenly at Dora and taking her measure without prejudice*].

DORA. Pleased to meet you. [*Juggins places the baby rocking-chair for her on Gilbey's right, opposite the Knoxes*]. Thank you. [*She sits*]. Bobby's given me the squiffer. Do you know what theyve been doing downstairs? Youd never guess. Theyve been trying to teach me table manners. The Lieutenant and Rudolph say I'm a regular pig. I'm sure I never knew there was anything wrong with me. But live and learn. [*To Gilbey*] Eh, old dear?

JUGGINS. Old dear is not correct, Miss Delaney. [*He retires to the end of the sideboard nearest the door*].

DORA. Oh get out! I must call a man something. He doesnt mind: do you, Charlie?

MRS GILBEY. His name isnt Charlie.

DORA. Excuse me. I call everybody Charlie.

JUGGINS. You mustnt.

DORA. Oh, if I were to mind you, I should have to hold my tongue altogether; and then how sorry youd be! Lord, how I do run on! Dont mind me, Mrs Gilbey.

KNOX. What I want to know is, whats to be the end of this? It's not for me to interfere between you and your son, Gilbey: he knows his own intentions best, no doubt, and perhaps has told them to you. But Ive my daughter to look after; and it's my duty as a parent to have a clear understanding about her. No good is ever done by beating about the bush. I ask Lieutenant – well, I dont speak French; and I cant pronounce the name –

MARGARET. Mr Duvallet, father.

KNOX. I ask Mr Doovalley what his intentions are.

MARGARET. Oh, father: how can you?

DUVALLET. I'm afraid my knowledge of English is not enough to understand. Intentions? How?

MARGARET. He wants to know will you marry me.

MRS GILBEY. What a thing to say!
KNOX. Silence, miss.
DORA. Well, thats straight, aint it?

DUVALLET. But I am married already. I have two daughters.

KNOX [*rising, virtuously indignant*] You sit there after carrying on with my daughter, and tell me coolly youre married.

MARGARET. Papa: you really must not tell people that they sit there. [*He sits down again sulkily*].

DUVALLET. Pardon. Carrying on? What does that mean?

MARGARET. It means –

KNOX [*violently*] Hold your tongue, you shameless young hussy. Dont you dare say what it means.

DUVALLET [*shrugging his shoulders*] What does it mean, Rudolph?

MRS KNOX. If it's not proper for her to say, it's not proper for a man to say, either. Mr Doovalley: youre a married man with daughters. Would you let them go about with a stranger, as you are to us, without wanting to know whether he intended to behave honorably?

DUVALLET. Ah, madam, my daughters are French girls. That is

very different. It would not be correct for a French girl to go about alone and speak to men as English and American girls do. That is why I so immensely admire the English people. You are so free – so unprejudiced – your women are so brave and frank – their minds are so – how do you say? – wholesome. I intend to have my daughters educated in England. Nowhere else in the world but in England could I have met at a Variety Theatre a charming young lady of perfect respectability, and enjoyed a dance with her at a public dancing saloon. And where else are women trained to box and knock out the teeth of policemen as a protest against injustice and violence? [*Rising, with immense élan*] Your daughter, madam, is superb. Your country is a model to the rest of Europe. If you were a Frenchman, stifled in prudery, hypocrisy, and the tyranny of the family and the home, you would understand how an enlightened Frenchman admires and envies your freedom, your broadmindedness, and the fact that home life can hardly be said to exist in England. You have made an end of the despotism of the parent; the family council is unknown to you; everywhere in these islands one can enjoy the exhilarating, the soul-liberating spectacle of men quarrelling with their brothers, defying their fathers, refusing to speak to their mothers. In France we are not men: we are only sons – grown-up children. Here one is a human being – an end in himself. Oh, Mrs Knox, if only your military genius were equal to your moral genius – if that conquest of Europe by France which inaugurated the new age after the Revolution had only been an English conquest, how much more enlightened the world would have been now! We, alas, can only fight. France is unconquerable. We impose our narrow ideas, our prejudices, our obsolete institutions, our insufferable pedantry on the world by brute force – by that stupid quality of military heroism which shews how little we have evolved from the savage: nay, from the beast. We can charge like bulls; we can spring on our foes like gamecocks; when we are overpowered by treason, we can die fighting like rats. And we are foolish enough to be proud of it! Why should we be? Does the bull progress? Can you civilize the gamecock? Is there any future for the rat? We never fight intelligently: when we lose battles, it is because we have not sense enough to know when we are beaten. At Waterloo, had we known when we were beaten, we should have retreated; tried another plan; and won the battle. But no: we were too pigheaded to admit that there is anything impossible to a Frenchman: we were quite satisfied when our Marshals had six horses shot under them, and our stupid old grognards died fighting rather than surrender like reasonable beings. Think of your great Wellington: think of his inspiring words, when the lady asked him whether British soldiers ever ran away. 'All soldiers run away, madam,' he said; 'but if there are supports for them to fall back on it does not matter.' Think of your illustrious Nelson, always beaten on land, always victorious at sea, where his men could not run away. You are not dazzled and misled by false ideals of patriotic enthusiasm: your honest and sensible statesmen demand for England a two-power standard, even a three-power standard, frankly admitting that it is wise to fight three to one: whilst we, fools and braggarts as we are, declare that every Frenchman is a host in himself, and that when one Frenchman attacks three Englishmen he is guilty of an act of cowardice comparable to that of the man who strikes a woman. It is folly: it is nonsense: a Frenchman is not really stronger than a German, than an Italian, even than an Englishman. Sir: if all Frenchwomen were like your daughter – if all Frenchmen had the good sense, the power of seeing things as they really are, the calm judgment, the open mind, the philosophic grasp, the foresight and true courage, which are so natural to you as an Englishman that you are hardly conscious of possessing them, France would become the greatest nation in the world.

MARGARET. Three cheers for old England! [*She shakes hands with him warmly*].

BOBBY. Hurra-a-ay! And so say all of us.

Duvallet, having responded to Margaret's handshake with enthusiasm, kisses Juggins on both cheeks, and sinks into his chair, wiping his perspiring brow.

GILBEY. Well, this sort of talk is above me. Can you make anything out of it, Knox?

KNOX. The long and the short of it seems to be that he cant lawfully marry my daughter, as he ought after going to prison with her.

DORA. I'm ready to marry Bobby, if that will be any satisfaction.

GILBEY. No you dont. Not if I know it.

MRS KNOX. He ought to, Mr Gilbey.

GILBEY. Well, if thats your religion, Amelia Knox, I want no more of it. Would you invite them to your house if he married her?

MRS KNOX. He ought to marry her whether or no.

BOBBY. I feel I ought to, Mrs Knox.

GILBEY. Hold your tongue. Mind your own business.

BOBBY [*wildly*] If I'm not let marry her, I'll do something downright disgraceful. I'll enlist as a soldier.

JUGGINS [*sternly*] That is not a disgrace, sir.

BOBBY. Not for you, perhaps. But youre only a footman. I'm a gentleman.

MRS GILBEY. Dont dare to speak disrespectfully to Mr Rudolph, Bobby. For shame!

JUGGINS [*coming forward to the middle of the table*] It is not gentlemanly to regard the service of your country as disgraceful. It is gentlemanly to marry the lady you make love to.

GILBEY [*aghast*] My boy is to marry this woman and be a social outcast!

JUGGINS. Your boy and Miss Delaney will be inexorably condemned by respectable society to spend the rest of their days in precisely the sort of company they seem to like best and be most at home in.

KNOX. And my daughter? Whos to marry my daughter?

JUGGINS. Your daughter, sir, will probably marry the man she makes up her mind to marry. She is a lady of very determined character.

KNOX. Yes: if he'd have her with her character gone. But who would? Youre the brother of a duke. Would –

BOBBY. Whats that?
MARGARET. Juggins a duke!
DUVALLET. *Comment!*
DORA. What did I tell you?

KNOX. Yes: the brother of a duke: thats what he is. [*To Juggins*] Well, would you marry her?

JUGGINS. I was about to propose that solution of your problem, Mr Knox.

MRS GILBEY. Well, I never!
KNOX. D'ye mean it?
MRS KNOX. Marry Margaret!

JUGGINS [*continuing*] As an idle younger son, unable to support myself, or even to remain in the Guards in competition with the grandsons of American millionaires, I could not have aspired to Miss Knox's hand. But as a sober, honest, and industrious domestic servant, who has, I trust, given satisfaction to his employer [*he bows to Mr Gilbey*] I feel I am a man with a character. It is for Miss Knox to decide.

MARGARET. I got into a frightful row once for admiring you, Rudolph.

JUGGINS. I should have got into an equally frightful row myself, Miss, had I betrayed my admiration for you. I looked forward to those weekly dinners.

MRS KNOX. But why did a gentleman like you stoop to be a footman?

DORA. He stooped to conquer.

MARGARET. Shut up, Dora: I want to hear.

JUGGINS. I will explain; but only Mrs Knox will understand. I once insulted a servant. Rashly; for he was a sincere Christian. He rebuked me for trifling with a girl of his own class. I told him to remember what he was, and to whom he was speaking. He said God would remember. I discharged him on the spot.

GILBEY. Very properly.

KNOX. What right had he to mention such a thing to you?

MRS GILBEY. What are servants coming to?

MRS KNOX. Did it come true, what he said?

JUGGINS. It stuck like a poisoned arrow. It rankled for months. Then I gave in. I apprenticed myself to an old butler of ours who kept a hotel. He taught me my present business, and got me a place as footman with Mr Gilbey. If ever I meet that man again I shall be able to look him in the face.

MRS KNOX. Margaret: it's not on account of the duke: dukes are vanities. But take my advice; and take him.

MARGARET [*slipping her arm through his*] I have loved Juggins since the first day I beheld him. I felt instinctively he had been in the Guards. May he walk out with me, Mr Gilbey?

KNOX. Dont be vulgar, girl. Remember your new position. [*To Juggins*] I suppose youre serious about this, Mr – Mr Rudolph?

JUGGINS. I propose, with your permission, to begin keeping company this afternoon, if Mrs Gilbey can spare me.

GILBEY [*in a gust of envy, to Bobby*] Itll be long enough before youll marry the sister of a duke, you young good-for-nothing.

DORA. Dont fret, old dear. Rudolph will teach me high-class manners. I call it quite a happy ending: dont you, lieutenant?

DUVALLET. In France it would be impossible. But here – ah! [*kissing his hand*] la belle Angleterre!

EPILOGUE

Before the curtain. The Count, dazed and agitated, hurries to the 4 critics, as they rise, bored and weary, from their seats.

THE COUNT. Gentlemen: do not speak to me. I implore you to withhold your opinion. I am not strong enough to bear it. I could never have believed it. Is this a play? Is this, in any sense of the word, Art? Is it agreeable? Can it conceivably do good to any human being? Is it delicate? Do such people really exist? Excuse me, gentlemen: I speak from a wounded heart. There are private reasons for my discomposure. This play implies obscure, unjust, unkind reproaches and menaces to all of us who are parents.

TROTTER. Pooh! you take it too seriously. After all, the thing has amusing passages. Dismiss the rest as impertinence.

THE COUNT. Mr Trotter: it is easy for you to play the pococurantist. [*Trotter, amazed, repeats the first three syllables in his throat, making a noise like a pheasant*]. You see hundreds of plays every year. But to me, who have never seen anything of this kind before, the effect of this play is terribly disquieting. Sir: if it had been what people call an immoral play, I shouldnt have minded a bit. [*Vaughan is shocked*]. Love beautifies every romance and justifies every audacity. [*Bannal assents gravely*]. But there are reticences which everybody should respect. There are decencies too subtle to be put into words, without which human society would be unbearable. People could not talk to one another as those people talk. No child could speak to its parent: no girl could speak to a youth: no human creature could tear down the veils – [*Appealing to Vaughan, who is on his left flank, with Gunn between them*] Could they, sir?

VAUGHAN. Well, I dont see that.

THE COUNT. You dont see it! dont feel it! [*To Gunn*] Sir: I appeal to you.

GUNN [*with studied weariness*] It seems to me the most ordinary sort of old-fashioned Ibsenite drivel.

THE COUNT [*turning to Trotter, who is on his right, between him and Bannal*] Mr Trotter: will you tell me that you are not amazed, outraged, revolted, wounded in your deepest and holiest feelings by every word of this play, every tone, every implication; that you did not sit there shrinking in every fibre at the thought of what might come next?

TROTTER. Not a bit. Any clever modern girl could turn out that kind of thing by the yard.

THE COUNT. Then, sir, tomorrow I start for Venice, never to return. I must believe what you tell me. I perceive that you are not agitated, not surprised, not concerned; that my own horror (yes, gentlemen, horror – horror of the very soul) appears unaccountable to you, ludicrous, absurd, even to you, Mr Trotter, who are little younger than myself. Sir: if young people spoke to me like that, I should die of shame: I could not face it. I must go back. The world has passed me by and left me. Accept the apologies of an elderly and no doubt ridiculous admirer of the art of a bygone day, when there was still some beauty in the world and some delicate grace in family life. But I promised my daughter your opinion; and I must keep my word. Gentlemen: you are the choice and master spirits of this age: you walk through it without bewilderment and face its strange products without dismay. Pray deliver your verdict. Mr Bannal: you know that it is the custom at a Court Martial for the youngest officer present to deliver his judgment first; so that he may not be influenced by the authority of his elders. You are the youngest. What is your opinion of the play?

BANNAL. Well, whos it by?

THE COUNT. That is a secret for the present.

BANNAL. You dont expect me to know what to say about a play when I dont know who the author is, do you?

THE COUNT. Why not?

BANNAL. Why not! Why not!! Suppose you had to write about a play by Pinero and one by Jones! Would you say exactly the same thing about them?

THE COUNT. I presume not.

BANNAL. Then how could you write about them until you knew which was Pinero and which was Jones? Besides, what sort of play is this? thats what I want to know. Is it a comedy or a tragedy? Is it a farce or a melodrama? Is it repertory theatre tosh, or really straight paying stuff?

GUNN. Cant you tell from seeing it?

BANNAL. I can see it all right enough; but how am I to know how to take it? Is it serious, or is it spoof? If the author knows what his play is, let him tell us what it is. If he doesnt, he cant complain if I dont know either. *I*'m not the author.

THE COUNT. But is it a good play, Mr Bannal? Thats a simple question.

BANNAL. Simple enough when you know. If it's by a good author, it's a good play, naturally. That stands to reason. Who is the author? Tell me that; and I'll place the play for you to a hair's breadth.

THE COUNT. I'm sorry I'm not at liberty to divulge the author's name. The author desires that the play should be judged on its merits.

BANNAL. But what merits can it have except the author's merits? Who would you say it's by, Gunn?

GUNN. Well, who do you think? Here you have a rotten old-fashioned domestic melodrama acted by the usual stage puppets. The hero's a naval lieutenant. All melodramatic heroes are naval lieutenants. The heroine gets into trouble by defying the law (if she didnt get into trouble, thered be no drama) and plays for sympathy all the time as hard as she can. Her good old pious mother turns on her cruel father when he's going to put her out of the house, and says she'll go too. Then theres the comic relief: the comic shopkeeper, the comic shopkeeper's wife, the comic footman who turns out to be a duke in disguise, and the young scapegrace who gives the author his excuse for dragging in a fast young woman. All as old and stale as a fried fish shop on a winter morning.

THE COUNT. But –

GUNN [*interrupting him*] I know what youre going to say, Count. Youre going to say that the whole thing seems to you to be quite new and unusual and original. The naval lieutenant is a Frenchman who cracks up the English and runs down the French: the hackneyed old Shaw touch. The characters are second-rate middle class, instead of being dukes and millionaires. The heroine gets kicked through the mud: real mud. Theres no plot. All the old stage conventions and puppets without the old ingenuity and the old enjoyment. And a feeble air of intellectual pretentiousness kept up all through to persuade you that if the author hasnt written a good play it's because he's too clever to stoop to anything so commonplace. And you three experienced men have sat through all this, and cant tell me who wrote it! Why, the play bears the author's signature in every line.

BANNAL. Who?

GUNN. Granville-Barker, of course. Why, old Gilbey is straight out of The Madras House.

BANNAL. Poor old Barker!

VAUGHAN. Utter nonsense! Cant you see the difference in style?

BANNAL. No.

VAUGHAN [*contemptuously*] Do you know what style is?

BANNAL. Well, I suppose youd call Trotter's uniform style. But its not my style – since you ask me.

VAUGHAN. To me it's perfectly plain who wrote that play. To begin with, it's intensely disagreeable. Therefore it's not by Barrie, in spite of the footman, whos cribbed from The Admirable Crichton. He was an earl, you may remember. You notice, too, the author's offensive habit of saying silly things that have no real sense in them when you come to examine them, just to set all the fools in the house giggling. Then what does it all come to? An attempt to expose the supposed hypocrisy of the Puritan middle class in England: people just as good as the author, anyhow. With, of course, the inevitable improper female: the Mrs Tanqueray, Iris, and so forth. Well, if you cant recognize the author of that, youve mistaken your profession: thats all I have to say.

BANNAL. Why are you so down on Pinero? And what about that touch that Gunn spotted? the Frenchman's long speech. I believe it's Shaw.

GUNN. Rubbish!

VAUGHAN. Rot! You may put that idea out of your head, Bannal. Poor as this play is, theres the note of passion in it. You feel somehow that beneath all the assumed levity of that poor waif and stray, she really loves Bobby and will be a good wife to him.

Now Ive repeatedly proved that Shaw is physiologically incapable of the note of passion.

BANNAL. Yes, I know. Intellect without emotion. Thats right, I always say that myself. A giant brain, if you ask me; but no heart.

GUNN. Oh, shut up, Bannal. This crude medieval psychology of heart and brain – Shakespear would have called it liver and wits – is really schoolboyish. Surely weve had enough of secondhand Schopenhauer. Even such a played-out old back number as Ibsen would have been ashamed of it. Heart and brain, indeed!

VAUGHAN. You have neither one nor the other, Gunn. Youre dekkadent.

GUNN. Decādent! How I love that early Victorian word!

VAUGHAN. Well, at all events, you cant deny that the characters in this play are quite distinguishable from one another. That proves it's not by Shaw, because all Shaw's characters are himself: mere puppets struck up to spout Shaw. It's only the actors that make them seem different.

BANNAL. There can be no doubt of that: everybody knows it. But Shaw doesnt write his plays as plays. All he wants to do is to insult everybody all round and set us talking about him.

TROTTER [*wearily*] And naturally, here we are all talking about him. For heaven's sake, let us change the subject.

VAUGHAN. Still, my articles about Shaw –

GUNN. Oh, stow it, Vaughan. Drop it. What Ive always told you about Shaw is –

BANNAL. There you go, Shaw, Shaw, Shaw! Do chuck it. If you want to know my opinion about Shaw –

TROTTER } [*yelling*] { No, please, we dont.
VAUGHAN } [*yelling*] { Shut your head, Bannal.
GUNN } [*yelling*] { Oh do drop it.

The deafened Count puts his fingers in his ears and flies from the centre of the group to its outskirts, behind Vaughan.

BANNAL [*sulkily*] Oh, very well. Sorry I spoke, I'm sure.

TROTTER } [*beginning again simultaneously*] { Shaw –
VAUGHAN } [*beginning again simultaneously*] { Shaw –
GUNN } [*beginning again simultaneously*] { Shaw –

They are cut short by the entry of Fanny through the curtains. She is almost in tears.

FANNY [*coming between Trotter and Gunn*] I'm so sorry, gentlemen. And it was such a success when I read it to the Cambridge Fabian Society!

TROTTER. Miss O'Dowda: I was about to tell these gentlemen what I guessed before the curtain rose: that you are the author of the play. [*General amazement and consternation*].

FANNY. And you all think it beastly. You hate it. You think I'm a conceited idiot, and that I shall never be able to write anything decent.

She is almost weeping. A wave of sympathy carries away the critics.

VAUGHAN. No, no. Why, I was just saying that it must have been written by Pinero. Didnt I, Gunn?

FANNY [*enormously flattered*] Really?

TROTTER. I thought Pinero was much too popular for the Cambridge Fabian Society.

FANNY. Oh yes, of course; but still – Oh, did you really say that, Mr Vaughan?

GUNN. I owe you an apology, Miss O'Dowda. I said it was by Barker.

FANNY [*radiant*] Granville-Barker! Oh, you couldnt really have thought it so fine as that.

BANNAL. *I* said Bernard Shaw.

FANNY. Oh, of course it would be a little like Bernard Shaw. The Fabian touch, you know.

BANNAL [*coming to her encouragingly*] A jolly good little play, Miss O'Dowda. Mind: I dont say it's like one of Shakespear's – Hamlet or The Lady of Lyons, you know – but still, a firstrate little bit of work. [*He shakes her hand*].

GUNN [*following Bannal's example*] I also, Miss O'Dowda. Capital. Charming. [*He shakes hands*].

VAUGHAN [*with maudlin solemnity*] Only be true to yourself, Miss O'Dowda. Keep serious. Give up making silly jokes. Sustain the note of passion. And youll do great things.

FANNY. You think I have a future?

TROTTER. You have a past, Miss O'Dowda.

FANNY [*looking apprehensively at her father*] Sh-sh-sh!

THE COUNT. A past! What do you mean, Mr Trotter?

TROTTER [*to Fanny*] You cant deceive me. That bit about the police was real. Youre a Suffraget, Miss O'Dowda. You were on that Deputation.

THE COUNT. Fanny: is that true?

FANNY. It is. I did a month with Lady Constance Lytton; and I'm prouder of it than I ever was of anything or ever shall be again.

TROTTER. Is that any reason why you should stuff naughty plays down my throat?

FANNY. Yes: itll teach you what it feels like to be forcibly fed.

THE COUNT. She will never return to Venice. I feel now as I felt when the Campanile fell.

Savoyard comes in through the curtains.

SAVOYARD [*to the Count*] Would you mind coming to say a word of congratulation to the company? Theyre rather upset at having had no curtain call.

THE COUNT. Certainly, certainly. I'm afraid Ive been rather remiss. Let us go on the stage, gentlemen.

The curtains are drawn, revealing the last scene of the play and the actors on the stage. The Count, Savoyard, the critics, and Fanny join them, shaking hands and congratulating.

THE COUNT. Whatever we may think of the play, gentlemen, I'm sure you will agree with me that there can be only one opinion about the acting.

THE CRITICS. Hear hear! [*They start the applause*].

AYOT ST LAWRENCE, *March 1911*

Bernard Shaw in Penguin: A Selection

ANDROCLES AND THE LION
THE APPLE CART
BACK TO METHUSELAH
THE DOCTOR'S DILEMMA
HEARTBREAK HOUSE
JOHN BULL'S OTHER ISLAND
LAST PLAYS
(*In Good King Charles's Golden Days/Buoyant Billions/ Farfetched Fables/Shakes Versus Shav/Why She Would Not*)
MAJOR BARBARA
MAN AND SUPERMAN
MISALLIANCE *and* THE FASCINATING FOUNDLING
PLAYS EXTRAVAGANT
(*Too True To Be Good/The Simpleton of the Unexpected Isles/ The Millionairess*)
PLAYS UNPLEASANT
(*Widowers' Houses/The Philanderer/Mrs Warren's Profession*)
PYGMALION
SAINT JOAN
SELECTED ONE ACT PLAYS
THREE PLAYS FOR PURITANS
(*The Devil's Disciple/Caesar and Cleopatra/ Captain Brassbound's Conversion*)

Also published
THE INTELLIGENT WOMAN'S GUIDE TO SOCIALISM, CAPITALISM, SOVIETISM AND FASCISM